estherpress

Books for Courageous Women

T0006424

ESTHER PRESS VISION

Publishing diverse voices that encourage and equip women to walk courageously in the light of God's truth for such a time as this.

BIBLICAL STATEMENT OF PURPOSE

"For if you keep silent at this time, relief and deliverance will rise for the Jews from another place, but you and your father's house will perish. And who knows whether you have not come to the kingdom for such a time as this?"

Esther 4:14 (ESV)

What people are saying about …

SHE'S NOT YOUR ENEMY

"In a world that regularly pits women against each other, we need brave souls who will fight for empathy, compassion, and celebration—rather than live in scarcity and competition. Jenn Schultz invites the reader to be brave by understanding who our true Enemy actually is and by teaching us all how to better honor the women in our lives (including ourselves). You will enjoy learning from Jenn's generous and bighearted outlook."

Aubrey Sampson, author of *Known, The Louder Song,* and *Overcomer*

"Jenn Schultz writes with a beautiful transparency that is both refreshing and inviting. This book takes us on a journey to assured confidence in Christ's love for us and provides indisputable clarity on who our real Enemy is."

Jamie Watkins, mental wellness speaker and coach, author of *My Peace of Happy*

"If you've ever struggled with comparison or your worth, this book is absolutely for you. In a world that tries to tell us that our identity is found in the numbers we have on social media, the rooms we're invited to, and the tables we sit at, Jenn offers us a refreshing and much-needed message—one that is sure to free you from the insecurities you've been grappling with your whole life—and invites you into a new season of life with fresh confidence in who you are and who God calls you to be. This book will be one to pick up again and again."

Alexandra Hoover, bestselling author of *Eyes Up,* Bible teacher, ministry leader, and speaker

"This book is for anyone who has ever felt overlooked, discounted, or cast off to the sidelines. Take heart—you're about to encounter some hard-earned and beautiful truth within these pages. Jenn strikes a masterful blend of wisdom, vulnerability, and practicality as she lovingly leads her readers through the battlefield of comparison and shows them how to step fully into the spaces God has for them."

Hannah Brencher, author of *Fighting Forward* and *Come Matter Here*

"Now more than ever, our insecurities manipulate and distract us from our true identities in God. In *She's Not Your Enemy*, Jenn takes a unique and all-encompassing perspective in helping you identify and overcome the lack we all think we have by pointing you to the truth that fills up and redirects us to our kingdom-given purpose. Her words encourage and empower you to live present to God in your life instead of in others. This book will set you free."

Tabitha Panariso, writer and therapist

"Jenn has a gift for helping us identify and battle our thought struggles with generous grace and a gentle sense of humor. *She's Not Your Enemy* is about so much more than comparison with other women; it's about escaping the hamster wheel of performance and perfection to find peace, joy, and confidence in who God says we *already are* in Christ. Packed with scriptural insights and practical pointers, this book helps us change the way we relate to God and to ourselves, which ends up transforming the way we relate to others—because when other women cease to feel like enemies, they are free to become our friends."

Elizabeth Laing Thompson, author of *When a Friendship Falls Apart*,
All the Feels, All the Feels for Teens, and the When God Says series

SHE'S
NOT
YOUR
ENEMY

SHE'S NOT YOUR ENEMY

Conquering Our Insecurities So We Can Build God's Kingdom Together

JENN SCHULTZ

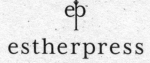

esther press

Books for Courageous Women
from David C Cook

SHE'S NOT YOUR ENEMY
Published by Esther Press,
an imprint of David C Cook
4050 Lee Vance Drive
Colorado Springs, CO 80918 U.S.A.

Integrity Music Limited, a Division of David C Cook
Brighton, East Sussex BN1 2RE, England

Esther Press, David C Cook, and related logos are trademarks of David C Cook.

ISBN 978-0-8307-8525-4
eISBN 978-0-8307-8526-1

© 2023 Jenn Schultz
Published in association with the literary agency of WordServe
Literary Group, Ltd., www.wordserveliterary.com.

The Team: Susan McPherson, Stephanie Bennett, Michael Ross,
Judy Gillispie, James Hershberger, Susan Murdock
Cover Design: Micah Kandros

Printed in the United States of America
First Edition 2023

1 2 3 4 5 6 7 8 9 10

052423

To my three:
May you always be confident
in who God made you to be,
play your own special part,
and cheer each other on.

And to my husband, for your
unfailing support and strength.

Contents

Know Your Enemy

You and I have been trained to spot the villain.

It starts young, in the tales we absorb growing up: The princess and the sorceress. The mermaid and the sea witch. The pigs and the wolf. The peasant and the giant.

Our beautifully diverse societies find commonality in the cultural tradition of storytelling. Stories have been around nearly as long as humans have. Communities would gather around revered leaders who recited, sang, and danced stories. The tales they wove would pass down history or personal experiences, contemplate big questions, share wisdom, entertain, and teach lessons.

Some of those same tales live on in school, where your teacher may have asked, "What's the moral?" Even the youngest children can identify the people we should try to imitate and the ones we should avoid.

The villains.

These days, storytelling is extended to movies, books, theater, and television. Sometimes you can identify the villain right from the start. Certain cues can usually tip you off to the "bad guy," like a distinctive theme song, a sinister smile or laugh, or exaggerated physical features or makeup.

Other times, the bad guys are revealed more in the climax of the plot or only at the very end. If you're like me, you might play detective and try to figure it out before the plot reveals him or her. (It drives my husband crazy, especially since I tend to figure it out. That's probably why he doesn't watch *Only Murders in the Building* with me.)

These villains clash with the heroes in more ways than one: not just in appearance but in motivations, characteristics, and choices. The more that unravels about their stories, the more we understand their reasons, even if we don't always agree with them.

Recently, there's been a growing trend in entertainment: an attempt to understand and even embrace the "misunderstood" villain. Movies that tell their side of the story via a redemptive-origin story are becoming more popular, with main characters such as Maleficent and Cruella de Vil.

The villains are becoming more human. The lines are blurring. We're questioning the characters we thought we knew.

If there's anything I hope for you to take out of the book you're holding, it's this: A very clear picture of who your enemy is. And who it is not.

Meet the Enemy

Paul seemed to sense there would be some confusion on the point of whom we are fighting against. Ephesians 6:11–12 tells us to "put on the full armor of God, so that you can take your stand against the devil's schemes. *For our struggle is not against flesh and blood, but against the rulers, against the authorities, against the powers of this dark world and against the spiritual forces of evil in the heavenly realms.*"

As Christians, our fight isn't with people but with evil forces and authorities—all under the direction of one in particular. To fight the real Enemy, we have to be strongly aware of his character, his game plan, and the tricks he uses to cause problems for us.

Let's take a closer look at his character.

The real villain is insatiable. Power-hungry, he wants all that God has and nothing less. He is wildly jealous of our connection with our Father and the fact that we are made in God's image. His language is lies. He is corrupt, angry, and on a mission.

The real Enemy's goal is to keep us divided from a generous, healing, loving, and engaging Creator. He wants to make sure we never experience the peace, grace, and joy that God abundantly has for us. He doesn't want us to connect with the God who knows us intimately, loves us deeply, and breaks down barriers to invite us into reconciliation and relationship.

Our Enemy wants us to be skeptical of God instead of sustained by him. He wants us worrying about what God is withholding from us rather than wondering at all the good things God gives us. He likes to see us relying on ourselves, sitting in our shame, and being defined by our worst mistakes and biggest flaws.

When it comes to others, he wants us to be suspicious and guarded. He prefers us fighting and scraping for our portion in a system where there seems to be only so much to go around. He finds joy in seeing us interact in merely transactional relationships as they benefit us, not engaging with one another in collaboration and mutual understanding.

Our Enemy wants us to be more concerned with proving ourselves, making ourselves known, and gathering the most and the best of everything. In that condition, we wouldn't have time or space for God, much less others.

Your enemy is not, as you might think, the woman who threatens your position at work or in your social group. It's not the one who talks about you behind your back or argues with you about the pettiest things. It's not the one who seems to have it all together, making you feel inferior. It's not even the woman in the mirror.

Your one true Enemy goes by many names—the Accuser, the Devil, Lucifer—and is sometimes even disguised as an angel of light. His most commonly used name, Satan, literally translates to "adversary," an opponent or enemy. And he'll stop at nothing to not only destroy your relationship with God but also burn bridges with the women around you.

Why? Because God designed people with community in mind. When Satan messes with our unity, then the good plans and purposes God has for us to build his kingdom, working together using the gifts and talents he's given us, will be wasted and lost in a battle of competition and discord. Just the way the Enemy planned it.

The Enemy at Work

The Devil has some results to show for his efforts. It's especially evident and growing among the youngest generations, but if we're honest, it resonates at any age.

Our Comparison with Others Using Social Media Is Negatively Affecting Our Mental and Physical Health

A major study presented in a book titled *Young People, Social Media and Health* made this stunning statement: Young people are "manufacturing their wellbeing through social media," using platforms and online interactions to fill needs that are not being met offline (being "liked," for example).[1] Once I read that phrase, it resonated deeply within me, although I'm way past the days of textbooks and lockers. Students aren't the only ones facing this problem; it happens in every life stage.

Higher levels of social media use (and consequently, social comparison against highly curated and not always accurate social media feeds) are leading to low self-esteem, depression, unhealthy physical activity, eating disorders, and body image issues.[2]

We Are Obsessed with Perfection and Meritocracy

In a world where your value is directly correlated with your rank and achievements, our culture is full of people constantly trying to prove themselves. We try to meet the world's demands and find its approval, and then any failure to do so is a reflection of our inadequacy and our inferiority. Perfectionism is increasing among younger generations, who are being introduced to competition at school, at work, online, and more.[3]

An article for the Conversation titled "How Perfectionism Became a Hidden Epidemic among Young People" says: "This is a culture which preys on insecurities and amplifies imperfection, impelling young people to focus on their personal deficiencies. As a result, some young people brood chronically about how they should behave, how they should look, or what they should own."[4]

The brooding, manic performance and anxiety over social rank and achievements is resulting in depression, body image issues, eating disorders, suicidal thoughts, and even death.[5]

We Fear Scarcity

On a similar note, we can measure our worth by what we have (or what we don't). A third of teens and a quarter of young adults are experiencing anxiety over what they think they should have gained or achieved by now. We feel behind the curve, lacking in what's important, and fearful.[6]

In an NBC news article, Michelle Chen states, "Capitalism's underlying system of social norms over-inflates the value of wealth and reduces personal worth to external achievements and credentials."[7]

In other words, it sometimes feels like your value only lies in what you have to show for it.

We Are Getting Lonelier

A 2019 study by YouGov America shows that 30 percent of Millennials feel lonely and 22 percent say they have *no* friends. In another study conducted in 2018, 43 percent of Americans felt a form of isolation and like their relationships were not significant. Generation Z scored the highest for loneliness.[8]

Maybe we'll try to brush it off and say that loneliness is not that big of a deal. We can get by on our own, right? But take note—biologically, loneliness can increase the likelihood of an earlier death by 26 percent. Our bodies react to loneliness as they do to hunger and thirst, driving us to seek connection and leaving us desperate without it. As Lydia Denworth said, in a *Scientific American* study, "Our need to connect is apparently as fundamental as our need to eat."[9] We are truly wired to be in community with one another.

In *Built to Belong*, Natalie Franke sums up our society in this way: "We built our modern world not on the basis of belonging, but with a focus on individual autonomy, personal power, and guided by worldly measures of success."[10]

All in all, our obsession with what others have and achieve, our competitive drive to come out on top, and our fear of falling short or missing out are leading to serious health and mental issues. We are more lonely, anxious, depressed, and insecure in our overly connected (yet disconnected), overachieving world. Our identities are caught up in the wrong criteria, and it's affecting our relationships with others.

This is not the story God has written for us.

Compare and Contrast

Another thing we learn fairly early in school is this: comparing and contrasting.

You've heard the following saying again and again. It's probably come up on your social media feed more than once. The words are attributed to Theodore Roosevelt, but no one knows where they originated:

"Comparison is the thief of joy."

I'll be blunt: this quote stresses me out. *Oh, is that all? Just stop comparing, huh? Go ahead and tell me how, and sure, I'll stop!*

Here's the thing: we are *wired* to make comparisons—to notice our similarities and to acknowledge our differences. Leon Festinger first studied and coined the term "social comparison," finding in his research that we use comparisons to figure out where we fit in with the people around us, fill a core need to find out where we belong, and inspire ourselves to make decisions in our own lives.[11]

Comparison comes naturally with observation, which comes naturally with, you know, *life*. It's not something we flip on and off. Kids are expert comparers, readily weighing out who got more Halloween candy or the better sticker from the cashier at the store. In adults, it's more subtle. You might notice another woman on the street and immediately realize she is taller than you, has a different hair color, or is wearing similar sneakers.

Let's take it a step further. Maybe you strike up a conversation with another woman and find out you share a love for movies, Pilates, the beach, and coffee. *You're similar.*

But she prefers hazelnut lattes to your vanilla Americanos, grew up in a different country than you, is an early bird while you're a night owl, and works in a laboratory while you work at a desk. *You're different.*

We know how to compare and to contrast. And—*thank you, God*—we aren't all carbon copies of one another. We even have healthy competition and debate as part of our culture: an invitation to compare and contrast ideas, to agree or disagree, to set new records and achievements.

But then you note the name brand of her sneakers as opposed to your knockoffs, feel sensitive about how put together she looks while you're wearing sweats, and sense some insecurity about the job she has that required more degrees than yours.

The problem doesn't lie in the comparison. The problem is when we use the comparison to measure our worth. Comparison becomes unhealthy when it leads to social-ranking competition instead of kingdom-building cooperation.

Rather than simply acknowledging similarities or differences, we measure ourselves next to that person and rank ourselves on a ladder of how well or poorly we perceive the other person to be doing. This ranking establishes our identity and worth in our minds. Comparison becomes about what we gain or lose rather than about our relationship to the other person.

James 3:13–16 talks about this problem, saying this:

> Who is wise and understanding among you? Let them show it by their good life, by deeds done in the humility that comes from wisdom. But if you harbor *bitter envy* and *selfish ambition* in your hearts, do not boast about it or deny the truth. Such "wisdom" does not come down from heaven but is earthly, unspiritual, demonic. For where you have envy and selfish ambition, there you find disorder and every evil practice.

The problem is not just about our own issues of feeling jealous or trying to come out on top. They burn us too, individually. But the original language indicates that this is an issue that negatively affects the kingdom of God as a whole, creating rivalry and divisions.

The greatest harm doesn't come from individual feelings but rather from the disunity that unhealthy comparison brings to the body of Christ.

The Greek words for "bitter envy" are πικρὸν (*pikron*) ζῆλον (*zélon*), which mean "malignant zeal" or "heat." It's the devotion that should be reserved for God that is instead poisoned by antagonism or rottenness. The word for "bitter" also implies something acrid, a corrosive material.[12]

The Greek word for "selfish ambition" is ἐριθεία (*eritheia*),[13] which I define as conspiring or scheming in a way that is intended to divide.

> *In the face of Satan's lies—which are his native language and his main tool against us—it's time to armor up.*

No wonder this Scripture warns that these qualities bring "disorder and every evil practice." Satan is manipulating us with lies so we can become agents that dissolve and divide the church, whether we realize it or not.

We blame our division on social media or culture or sometimes even other people, but the truth is, these things only magnify the insecurities and feelings of inadequacy already at play within us—almost like those awful bathroom mirrors that not only light up your blemishes but warp them, making them look three times bigger in size.

How do we deal with the Enemy and the spiritual forces he works against us?

> Put on the full armor of God, so that when the day of evil comes, you may be able to stand your ground, and after you have done everything, to stand. Stand firm then, with the belt of truth buckled around your waist, with the breastplate of righteousness in place, and with your feet fitted with the readiness that comes from the gospel of peace. In addition to all this, take up the shield of faith, with which you can extinguish all the flaming arrows of the

evil one. Take the helmet of salvation and the sword of the Spirit,
which is the word of God. (Eph. 6:13–17)

To summarize: In the face of Satan's lies—which are his native language and
his main tool against us—it's time to armor up.

Good Theology

Researchers studying patterns of exclusion in the classroom made an interesting
discovery: children often imitate the example set by their teachers.[14]

When teachers directly or indirectly generate an atmosphere of heavy competition in class, students are more likely to exclude those who somehow get in the way
of achieving their goals. The result? Some children are left behind, especially those
with learning difficulties or disabilities. It's also important to note that children
tend to imitate their teachers, treating other students as they see the teachers do. If
teachers display belittling or impatience, these attitudes grow and spread.

On the other hand, in a classroom that values diversity and inclusion, students
are more likely to show empathy and support for one another, even appreciating one
another's differences.

How children in a classroom view the teacher affects how they treat one another.

How we view our heavenly Father affects how we treat one another in this world.

If we're going to tackle competition and unhealthy comparison in our lives, we
need some good theology: a perspective of God's character that is based on truth,
not determined by what we feel at the time or based on the world around us. Our
view of God—who he is and who he says we are—makes all the difference in how
we interact with those around us.

With God, there is no question about his good and perfect nature, no bad
example to be spoken of. Here is the constant, unfailing truth: Our God is not a
God of impatience, frustration, short temper, favoritism, unhealthy demands, or

exclusion. He's a God who invites us in, values each of us the way he made us, and models love, joy, peace, patience, kindness, goodness, faithfulness, gentleness, and self-control. Every single day.

I, for one, haven't always viewed him that way. More often, I've viewed God suspiciously, anxious about earning his approval and devastated when I felt he wasn't with me or didn't support me (especially when he seemed to be blessing someone else). With my eyes set on proving myself, I hurt and excluded others, felt paranoid about my own status with God, and scrambled for control over my circumstances.

> Our view of God—who he is and who he says we are—makes all the difference in how we interact with those around us.

In Matthew 25, Jesus tells a story about perspective. Here's my paraphrase: A master, preparing to leave for a journey, gives three servants gold "each according to his ability" (v. 15). When he returns, the first servant joyfully approaches him with ten bags instead of five, having put the money to work and earned the extra. "Great job! You are an excellent servant. Because you've done well with a little responsibility, I'll put you in charge of more. Come join me to celebrate!"

The second servant has the same joy, with two extra bags of gold to add to the two he'd been given. The master expresses the same response. (Side note: What kind of wealthy, powerful ruler invites the help to celebrate with him? One who is more like a generous father than a stingy boss.)

But the third servant approaches solemnly. "You aren't honorable and don't have much integrity. You steal what others have planted and reap the benefit of that. So I was scared, and I hid what you gave me in the ground. At least I'm giving it back to you—here." Whoa. Do these three even work for the same guy?

Good theology *matters*. It's the driving force behind everything we do. If we view God as he is—kind and generous—then serving him is a joy, and we will easily make decisions that honor him and treat others the same way he treats us. But if we think of him as sneaky, demanding, self-indulgent, harsh, and judgmental, then we respond accordingly, with fear, hesitation, and skepticism. We will self-protect.

You and I will each stand before God someday and give an account of how we used what he gave us in this world. It won't be about what she did or didn't do. We'd better have our perspective correct about who God is, long before we even get to that point.

What's Next?

How do we combat the real Enemy? How do we embrace the blessings and assignments God has for us while cheering each woman on for what he has for her and not letting the two get tangled and twisted?

The solution is not to work harder, or to empower ourselves, or to fall for any other trick Satan tries in order to get us to focus on an idol that isn't God. This isn't something we shape up and fix.

This is about wholeheartedly embracing and planting ourselves in who God says we are. It's about embracing our own unique gifts, experiences, and even flaws so that we can be stronger together and can play the roles God intended for us.

In this book, we will address all the women whom we confuse as the Enemy:

> The one who overlooks you
>
> The one who has the thing you most want
>
> The one who fights against you

The one dealing with chaos and discouragement

The one who doesn't believe what you believe

The one who is winning at life

The one who is hard to relate and connect to

The one who needs more than what you feel you can give

The one in the mirror who is never enough

We're going to address our unhealthy theology, holding it up to the light and the truth, and turn our attention to what God says about himself and about us—because he is completely trustworthy, faithful, holy, and honest. Having an accurate view of who he is paves the way for confidence in our own walks, and it sets us up for cooperation with those God has put around us.

The message of this book is not an overly simplified cliché, like "just stop comparing." If the issue isn't really between you and her, then the answer isn't "just stop."

The Enemy is Satan. The problem is that he wants us divided and discouraged. The solution is setting straight our perspective of God and how he sees us.

Let's Do This

Let me back up a minute and introduce myself. I'm Jenn. In the coming pages, I'll be your tour guide.

Just so you know, I'm no relationship expert, which is a good thing because unhealthy comparison isn't a relational issue. It's an identity problem. It has everything to do with how we perceive God and how we think he views us. The way we view and treat others and the way we experience life with them flows from our relationship with God, first and foremost.

I'm writing as someone vulnerable to unhealthy comparison and competitiveness. Someone who regularly faces off with her own identity and insecurity and inadequacy issues. I'm writing as someone who is searching for answers too.

After years of undoing the lies I used to believe about God and finding the freedom that comes from grace, I'm convinced that knowing God and taking him at his word makes the difference. Through our faith in Jesus, we can disarm the power of the Devil, right along with the lies we've been fed, as well as our sins *and* our struggles. And I'm confident that when we do this, we'll discover how much better we are together. Then we are free to each do our part: use our God-given talents and take on our God-given roles to build God's incredible kingdom.

> Speaking the truth in love, we will grow to become in every respect the mature body of him who is the head, that is, Christ. From him the whole body, joined and held together by every supporting ligament, grows and builds itself up in love, as each part does its work. (Eph. 4:15–16)

Throughout This Book

- We will face the lies the Enemy feeds us, take them before God, and work them out between him and us. We'll explore potential challenges we may face along the way: insecurity (lacking confidence and feeling uncertain about ourselves), which leads to feelings of inadequacy (questioning our overall worth or whether we're good enough), and ends in isolation and sometimes depression or anxiety.

- Together, we'll take the courageous steps that can help us grow toward maturity, leaving behind the things that divide. Only then will we be equipped to face the women God puts in our paths, without competition, envy, or selfish ambition. We will no longer look to them to prove our worth, our security, and our confidence.

- In each chapter, we'll turn to Scripture for truth and guidance, through which God defeats unhealthy thinking and breaks destructive cycles (2 Cor. 10:5).

- Along with God's Word, each chapter includes practical tools for combatting inadequacy, competition, imposter syndrome, bitterness, and jealousy in your life. We need to use every tool in our arsenal to shift our mindset to one of healthy cooperation—one where we are better together, working alongside each other to benefit others and glorify God.

- The end of each chapter provides a journaling section called "Let's Do This," along with key questions to help you "work it out" on your own or with a group. Here you will explore how God is speaking specifically to *you*. The next page will have you thinking in threes to help you move forward: three truths you know about God from that chapter (include Scripture if you can!), three things you're grateful for, and three small steps you can take in this area of life.

- You'll also find accompanying **videos**, in which I will guide you through specific action steps to help you resist the true Enemy. This video content is free to you and can be viewed alone or with a group. Access the videos by visiting the link or scanning the QR code on the next page.

As we take this journey together, we will discover how to:

1. Nurture more empathy, compassion, and love for the women we may have labeled as the enemy, finally realizing that they too may share our struggles with insecurity, inadequacy, and isolation.

2. Better understand comparison and find relief from competition with a drive toward cooperation.

3. Find practical steps toward conquering the lie of inadequacy and discover our unique offering to the world, working in community with other women rather than in competition.

Let's walk in the freedom we have in Christ and break free from the lies we've been fed. With the characters in their proper places, let's see where God's story for our lives goes.

Access the Videos Here
Link: DavidCCook.org/access
Access code: NotYourEnemy
Or scan this QR code:

Chapter 1

The Woman Who Doesn't Include You

Rejected. Overlooked. Dismissed. Ignored. Uninvited. Excluded. There's a certain heartbreak reserved for being left out.

Scrolling through Instagram, you spot photos from a girls' trip you weren't invited to.

You find yourself the awkward one out in a discussion as the rest of the circle shares experiences you cannot relate to.

"You're not the right fit for us," the email says, after multiple rounds of a job interview process.

Everyone in the room is already midconversation, and no one notices you or invites you to join.

Someone makes a joke at your expense, and you go from being inside the group to being the outlier.

Someone who was your friend yesterday wants nothing to do with you today.

You find out that you have been the topic of conversation around the workplace—and not in a good way.

Just a few of my personal experiences through the years. Maybe you can relate?

It's not a coincidence that it hurts. Rejection is a pain you can actually feel in your body, because social pain and physical pain activate the brain in the same places.[1] The neurons run through the same wiring and can overlap and affect one another. So that stinging, aching, or sharp sensation? It's valid. It hurts. And it's not about simply "getting over" those painful feelings of rejection.

Cliques and social ranking start young, in childhood and the teen years, and few of us escape it. Movies capture it well.

The lunch tables are unofficially assigned to each carefully categorized group. Who hasn't experienced that anxious feeling in their stomach while entering the school cafeteria, scanning the crowd for an empty seat near a familiar face?

Uncomfortable wallflowers sit on the sidelines at the dances. Or stay home completely. I was too bashful in school to attend most social events, out of fear of not knowing whom to hang with and being left alone. (I made it to senior prom and maybe one or two football games. That was basically it.)

The important titles and seats are reserved for the most popular. It feels crushing to be overlooked in class or at after-school activities simply because you're not on the inside track.

We leave behind many things from school—fortunately—but social ranking isn't one of them. It spreads into college. It seeps into our social circles. It affects who you talk to in the staff room or at the coffee station. You can spot it on the playground, among moms with diaper bags and strollers. Okay, let's be honest here. It can even cause deep divides in the one place that's supposed to be safe and inclusive: church.

Why does rejection hurt so much? And if it's so painful, why do we in turn reject or exclude others?

Because it's a two-way street, right? We are rejected, and we reject. We decide whom we want to be around and whom we don't. We intentionally and unintentionally leave people out.

We're all wounded, and we all inflict wounds.

The woman who excludes you is the one who didn't include you on the invitation list. She's the one who saw your text message and started to reply with those three punishing dots (because, apparently, we all need that much insight into when and how people are responding to us) and then disappeared. She's the one who is well into the group conversation but doesn't ask for your opinion, the one who started a morning walking group but didn't send you the details, the one who makes a snide comment about you to make everyone else laugh.

Sometimes she does it mindlessly, by accident. Sometimes it's intentional and overt. And then sometimes it's somewhere in the middle—not purposefully hurting any feelings but honestly not making an effort either.

Is this woman the enemy? Am I the enemy?

A Self-Fulfilling Prophecy

Invisibility became my superpower. But it wasn't always that way.

Up until first grade or so, I was loud and outgoing. Especially at church, surrounded by people who felt like family, it seemed like the safest place for me to be completely myself. I could be loud and silly, make faces and sing and dance, participate wholeheartedly without holding back—because the people around me were *my* people.

One day I was doing my thing around a group of friends—probably running around and yelling or something, acting goofy. That was when someone declared before our whole group, "You are so *weird*." Everyone giggled. I paused, and then giggled along too. You never want to be on the outside of the joke, even if you *are* the joke.

For a long time, the moment stuck with me, which still sounds absolutely ridiculous when I say it on paper or out loud. Why should it? Someone could have said or done a hundred things that were a lot more painful. Why did my mind keep hold of that one moment? After steady bouts of insecurity and social anxiety, it hit me years later: it wasn't the label that bothered me but rather the concept it had planted firmly within my mind—*You are the odd one out. You don't belong. And you didn't even realize it. How humiliating for you.*

Somewhere in the back of my mind, a running track started on a low volume. *You're not like everyone else. You don't fit in. There's something wrong with you.* And so, in an attempt to keep people from seeing me as the unusual one, I tried not to give them any ammunition. I grew quieter and quieter, the invisible girl in the back row. In school, I avoided the teacher's gaze, hoping not to have to answer questions. I hated group projects and presentations. With the small circle of people I trusted, I could be silly and less guarded; otherwise I ducked my head and stayed quiet.

I questioned myself constantly. *Is this what a normal person would do? What do these people think of me?*

And then it came back around full circle. It turns out that making yourself invisible leads to—surprise, surprise—people not noticing you. I'd go from one minute hoping no one would look at me to feeling hurt and left out the next. I wanted to prove I could handle being on my own, while secretly hoping someone would talk to me.

One day in a new class in college, I sat by myself and didn't talk to anyone. Then for an icebreaker, our teacher had us introduce ourselves to one another and eventually take turns saying everyone's name. We went around in a circle, and most of my classmates had forgotten my name just as quickly as they'd learned it. I fulfilled my own prophecy. I'd made myself forgettable.

Are there moments when seeds were planted that made you question your belonging? Maybe it was an accusation someone made, a lack of invitation, a misunderstanding, an act of discrimination, an offhand remark, or a joke at your expense. It could have been a friend, family member, or someone on the street. Maybe they meant it to inflict harm, or maybe it was unwitting. Either way, those weedy seeds can have a whole field day in your mind. (Or weeks, months, or *years*.)

We want to be liked, accepted, and included. We want to belong. It hurts deeply to be alienated or rejected, even if unintentionally.

But the enemy isn't the person who overlooks you, or calls you out, or leaves you out.

The Enemy's Game

As we grow and start to form opinions about our place in the world, in creep ranking and division. Our sinful natures make us crave approval, validation, and even superiority.

We know the drill. It feels good to be accepted and bad to be rejected. It feels nice when your place is secure ... and sometimes even more so when someone else's place is not.

In her book, *The Moment of Lift: How Empowering Women Changes the World*, Melinda French Gates says, "Overcoming the need to create outsiders is our greatest challenge as human beings. It is the key to ending deep inequality."[2]

I think we can all relate to that. Where does this need to create outsiders come from?

A Desire for Power

Power is a sense of having the upper hand, a confidence that comes from feeling superior and being in control, yet an unstable feeling because it lasts only as long as you can maintain it. A desire for power becomes dangerous and debilitating toward the marginalized. We will do anything to have authority.

A Feeling of Unworthiness

Insecurity prompts us to bolster ourselves by feeling out how "well" we're doing compared to someone else. Maybe if someone has less than us—less power and stuff, fewer accomplishments and connections—then our holes of uncertainty will fill up, making us feel more confident.

A Fear of Scarcity

Having authority, we think, means less of a chance of being excluded ourselves. Instead, we scrape and fight to achieve rank, and it feels so earned that we dismiss others, who may not have had equal opportunity.

If we're being deeply honest, these traits are not exclusive to bullies and "mean girls" like we see in the movies. You and I struggle with the same sinful nature. We're all at risk. Satan wants to use these feelings within us to divide and disengage.

On the other hand, those points above are the same conclusions we're left with when we feel rejected: powerless, unworthy, lacking. These fears and insecurities grow as moments of exclusion happen, prompting us to reject others so that, maybe for a minute or two, we don't have to feel that way ourselves. And the cycle goes on.

It is possible to break this terrible cycle. Although it's painful, being rejected doesn't have to hold the power to crush you every time. The hurt doesn't have to be a visitor that stays rent-free, indefinitely. Rejection also doesn't have to breed rejection. There's another way to approach our own insecurities and fears instead of taking down others to boost our moods for a while.

> *The hurt doesn't have to be a visitor that stays rent-free, indefinitely.*

The Bad News …?

You're not going to like the first part. I don't either.

The Bible often calls us to do things we don't want to do, embrace truths that aren't comfortable or easy, and entrust ourselves to the wisdom of God—a wisdom that our human knowledge can't touch.

As with every heavy truth in the Scriptures, something for our good is waiting on the other side. Hope prevails. There's a silver lining in the cloud, because we have a Father who is the most powerful being in the universe and happens to work things for our good. But sometimes we have to start with the rain and work our way through.

Here's the hard truth: we were never meant to belong in this world. At least not as it is.

One day on a mountainside, early into a new ministry, a young carpenter from Nazareth spoke to a crowd and left them stunned. Who was this, to speak with so much authority, certainty, and confidence? He preached more powerfully than the teachers of the law—and yet didn't have the credentials and respect of those venerated men.

Let's zero in on one particular part of the Sermon on the Mount. The way Eugene Peterson's *The Message* phrases this passage feels particularly poignant to me:

> You're blessed when your commitment to God provokes persecution. The persecution drives you even deeper into God's kingdom.
>
> Not only that—count yourselves blessed every time people put you down or throw you out or speak lies about you to discredit me. What it means is that the truth is too close for comfort and they are uncomfortable. You can be glad when that happens—give a cheer, even!—for though they don't like it, *I* do! And all heaven applauds. And know that you are in good company. My prophets and witnesses have always gotten into this kind of trouble. (Matt. 5:10–12)

What Jesus modeled for us is this: our Savior, the Son of God and most trustworthy friend, refused to let people define him. In multiple occurrences, Jesus' lack of concern for the approval of people is contrasted with the way the world around him thought. John in particular talks about this multiple times. In John 12:42–43, people who believed in Jesus wouldn't publicly support him, due to fear of what the Pharisees thought, "for they loved human praise more than praise from God." But when it came to Jesus, John 2:24–25 says that he didn't entrust himself to people, because he knew what was in their hearts.

As he prepared to go to the cross, Jesus told his closest disciples and all who would follow in their footsteps that we're not to expect any kind of warm welcome from the world when we choose God above all. In the end, he set the example for us by being rejected by both his enemies and even some of his closest friends.

> If the world hates you, keep in mind that it hated me first. If you belonged to the world, it would love you as its own. As it is, you

do not belong to the world, but I have chosen you out of the world. That is why the world hates you. Remember what I told you: "A servant is not greater than his master." If they persecuted me, they will persecute you also. (John 15:18–20)

If you have any experience with people-pleasing (like me), this passage might make you shiver a little bit. *Hated? You don't actually mean* hated, *do you, Jesus?* James draws the line in an even more blunt way in James 4:4–5:

You adulterous people, don't you know that friendship with the world means enmity against God? Therefore, anyone who chooses to be a friend of the world becomes an enemy of God. Or do you think Scripture says without reason that he jealously longs for the spirit he has caused to dwell in us?

That word *enmity*, to my mind, means hostility, or a state of active opposition. A battle stance, saying, "Come at me." Not a posture I want to take before the almighty God. I don't want to be on the side of the Enemy, thank you very much.

Paul concludes a strong admonishment in Galatians 1 with the words, "Am I now trying to win the approval of human beings, or of God? Or am I trying to please people? If I were still trying to please people, I would not be a servant of Christ" (v. 10).

Clearly, there is no option to fence-sit on this one. The goal of getting everyone's approval puts you in a fierce stance against God. Conversely, the world will reject you when you choose God instead of it.

It is impossible to please everyone and also please God. We're not meant to fit in with this world.

It doesn't end there, though. We have a Savior who walked this road first and walks it with us still. I love the way Dane Ortlund puts it in his book *Gentle and Lowly*: "If God sent his own Son to walk through the valley of condemnation, rejection, and hell, you can trust him as you walk through your own valleys on your way to heaven."[3]

The Best News

There is a place where you belong. It's the kingdom of God. You belong with the one who designed you and called you into being. That's where you were always meant to be.

In the beginning, in the first few days of stars and land and plants and fish and birds, humankind was created in the image of God. Male and female. And they were called "good." God spent time with his creation. He walked with them. There was nothing to get in the way.

Yet somehow our Enemy, Satan, wormed his way in and warped the beauty and goodness, twisting God's abundance and generosity and wisdom, even the character of God himself, into what felt like the very first rejection. He spoke to the first woman, planting seeds with a question and some blatant lies, and that seed took root, sprouting into all the things he didn't say. He didn't have to. The woman filled in the blanks: *You're not good enough. God knows you're not smart enough to handle this knowledge. That's why he's withholding it from you. You're excluded from this club.*

That's how the snake convinced the first woman, who was *made in God's image*, to believe she was on the outside and missing out. This woman, whom God called good, felt unworthy. And so she took care of the problem herself, with the bite of a forbidden fruit.

Her flawed perspective was handed down to all of us. This is the question we have to face every day as we battle our sinful natures: Will we trust God at his word about who he says we are, or will we take matters into our own hands to validate ourselves?

There is a place where you belong.
It's the kingdom of God.

Our relationship with God as it was meant to be is the one he had with the first man and woman in the garden, before a slithering snake came into the picture: partnering with each other and God. No competition or confusion. No grasping for power. Completely sustained by the One who shares with us everything we need and nothing we don't.

This is the kind of security and confidence I was desperately seeking as I sat invisibly in the back row. I knew about God and all the Scriptures that said he loves us. I could recite to you in a singsong voice various verses about Jesus, how his "yoke is easy" and his "burden is light," and what he did for all of us on the cross. But it took a long time to make the connection that I had nothing to do to prove myself or earn my place. His arms are wide open toward us. He invites us in. He accepts us.

Going back to our passage in John 15, just ahead of the warning that the world will hate his disciples, Jesus started with the best news: we are branches of his vine, part of him:

> As the Father has loved me, so have I loved you. Now remain in
> my love. If you keep my commands, you will remain in my love,
> just as I have kept my Father's commands and remain in his love. I
> have told you this so that my joy may be in you and that your joy

may be complete. My command is this: Love each other as I have loved you. (vv. 9–12)

We belong with Jesus. We belong with God. So your mission, should you choose to accept it? *To remain in him.* This brings the truest joy, and you can pass it on by loving others too. Our ultimate mission is to share this message of acceptance and belonging with those who are missing it.

> The LORD is with me; I will not be afraid.
>   What can mere mortals do to me?
> The LORD is with me; he is my helper.
>   I look in triumph on my enemies.

> It is better to take refuge in the LORD
>   than to trust in humans.
> It is better to take refuge in the LORD
>   than to trust in princes. (Ps. 118:6–9)

> The LORD is my light and my salvation—
>   whom shall I fear?
> The LORD is the stronghold of my life—
>   of whom shall I be afraid? (Ps. 27:1)

Accepted, loved, and invited by God—so who is allowed to make you afraid? No one. We have nothing to fear with him. May we take God at his every reliable word.

My heart breaks for the girl who felt she didn't belong. She ran on a hamster wheel of effort, hiding shame behind a mask of positivity, and often ended up missing the whole point. She missed out on chances to serve people as Jesus did, to actually hear and understand people who were hurting. All because she was hurting too and didn't know what to do with it.

I wish I could gently take her hands and tell her there was nothing she had to prove or earn with God. Her place with him is secure. His love for her is certain. His design and purpose for her are as they should be.

Maybe I can do that for you today. Let me take your hands and look straight into your eyes. You are secure and safe in God's love. Your incredible worth is not a question to the One who made you. No matter who tells you otherwise, who leaves you out or sends you packing, you are valuable and seen and known and loved. You are invited and welcome. You belong.

Rest confidently in this. And then go and break the cycles of rejection by inviting others in. Especially the ones who try to remain invisible.

Let's Do This

Make it a habit of going back to who God says you are with every rejection, big or small, by writing it down here. This is good practice for running back to the God who always welcomes you home. Remember that you belong with him. The rejections of the world hold less of a power over you when you do.

Work It Out

1. What seed was planted in your heart that made you feel like you didn't belong? Pray for God to redeem that seed and grow something beautiful there instead.

2. What characteristics would you choose to describe God? Do those characteristics make you respect him, or suspect him?

3. What's a place (past or present) where you feel like you belong? What makes it a safe place for you? Do you feel that way with God?

Three truths I know about God

+ _____
  _____

+ _____
  _____
  _____

+ _____
  _____
  _____

Three things I'm grateful for

+ _____
  _____

+ _____
  _____

+ _____
  _____

Three steps I can take moving forward

+ _____
  _____

+ _____
  _____

+ _____
  _____

Watch Video 1

Find the link on page 28.

Video Notes

Reflective Prayer

Prayer Requests

Praises

Chapter 2

The Woman Who Has What You Want

It was about time to cut the cake.

The games were over, and the appetizers on the kitchen table had been mostly devoured. Pink balloons and streamers hung everywhere. Pastel polka dots studded plates and napkins. Presents clustered around a chair that was draped with a sash reading "Mom-to-Be." A cacophony of chattering and laughing made a dull roar, the kind that always seems to grow wherever a group of women gather.

As slices were handed out, there was just enough commotion for me to slip out the side door without being noticed. The churning in my stomach wouldn't stop. Blinking back tears, I took deep breaths as I walked into the sunshine. *It's going to be okay. It's going to be okay.*

You could not be in attendance of this party without feeling a huge burst of joy for the guest of honor. She'd had trouble getting pregnant for years, and I was genuinely happy to see her prayer answered and heart's desire fulfilled.

But my own recent infertility diagnosis and an absolute terror about what it meant left me feeling alone and overwhelmed. My heart was torn between being happy for my friend and longing for what she had.

It was like this for almost two years. A friend would call with baby news, or my social media feed would fill with more pregnancy announcements, or party invitations would arrive in my inbox—and although I was happy for my friends, the pain was indescribable.

So many tears shed. So many negative tests in the trash can. Uncertainty. Terribly awkward and painful procedures. Prayers that seemed unanswered and unheard. An internal rebellion against joy for someone else as I went through my own struggle.

It's humiliating to admit that. Don't we all wish we could say that genuine happiness for someone else comes more easily than concern about our own lack? But sometimes the fear, doubt, and hurt clamp on to us and don't let go. As they grow, with some prompting from the Enemy, who manipulates us to question God's goodness and plan for us in it all, those feelings can even give way to envy, competition, and bitterness.

How do we reconcile our pain with a good God? How do we separate our own difficult journeys from others so that we can celebrate with them and cheer them on? How do we keep from falling into a destructive pattern of competition and envy when some other woman has what we want?

Cursed

In our fallen world, we experience what feels like curses all too often.

> The loved one you lose
> The bare ring finger
> The funds that don't come through
> The illness you didn't see coming

The countless negative pregnancy tests

The unjust accusation

The abrupt or excessive fallout

The career loss

The broken relationship

The pandemic that shuts the whole world down

The almost-but-not-quite-fulfilled dream

As women after God's heart, we desperately search for reason, answers, and relief. But the end result is usually just more questions. Why would God allow this heartache? Is he mad at me? What did I do wrong? How long will this take? Should I just give up hope?

Something that's particularly difficult to reconcile is this: *Why her and not me? Does God love, accept, and approve of her more than me?*

If you remember, feelings of rejection are painful because they follow the same wiring that feelings of physical pain go through. Here's the burning emotional conundrum that goes with this: sometimes the absence of a blessing can feel like a flat-out rejection from God. The God who is supposed to be loving, working for our well-being, leading us like a good shepherd. This stings especially if someone else is bursting with that very good news you've been waiting on.

Digging through the Bible for answers as I sorted through the pain, I kept going back to the stories where women were cursed with infertility. I hoped to quickly learn the lesson I must have needed so that I could graduate past this stage. At face value, these stories gave me confirmation that I must have done something truly deserving to be under that same curse. And all the women who managed to get pregnant? They were perfectly fine, totally loved by God.

Some days I made my pain about the other woman, whoever she was—a comparison game of why she deserved to be a mom and I didn't. Sometimes she won because of her surpassing good deeds or character; sometimes the catalog of my wrongs ruled me out. And sometimes, to be deeply honest, I thought I deserved this blessing and she didn't. My reasoning never made sense, any way I added it up.

It became painfully obvious that this wasn't really a battle between the other women and me. The battle was one-sided: me facing off against a God who wasn't geared up for battle against me at all.

The Rival

A woman in the Scriptures who could relate to us in the heartbreak of what she couldn't have was named Hannah. We find her story in 1 Samuel 1.

She was one of two wives of Elkanah, notably called out as the one who couldn't have children. The Bible actually says that "the LORD had closed her womb" (v. 5). She had the answer to her heart's desire: a resounding no. I'm guessing that in community with other wives, she stood out. I wonder if people called her cursed. Here's what verses 4–7 say:

> Whenever the day came for Elkanah to sacrifice, he would give portions of the meat to his wife Peninnah and to all her sons and daughters. But to Hannah he gave a double portion because he loved her, and the LORD had closed her womb. Because the LORD had closed Hannah's womb, her rival kept provoking her in order to irritate her. This went on year after year. Whenever Hannah went up to the house of the LORD, her rival provoked her till she wept and would not eat.

Whether you've read this passage once or a hundred times, you might gather that there was some competition between the two wives: the one who had children and the one who didn't, egged on by their husband, who seemed to love one more than the other. It might seem obvious—as though of course Peninnah is the enemy here, mercilessly provoking an innocent and grieving Hannah. But did you notice the wording there? "Her rival." Nowhere in those verses does it specifically identify Peninnah as the one who tormented Hannah.

Why does the Bible word it that way instead of deliberately naming names? Could "the rival" have been one of Peninnah's friends or someone from town who didn't let Hannah forget her misery? Could it have been Hannah's internal struggle with herself? It doesn't say.

The important thing here is this: whether or not Hannah had another person as a rival doesn't matter. The real rival at work was the exact same one at work from the beginning—the one who wanted to keep Hannah suspended in disbelief and discouragement so that her situation would never change. So that she'd never live out her purpose and become the mother to the prophet and last judge of Israel, Samuel.

Your true rival will do the same to you: stir up doubts about the goodness and capability of God, just as he did in Eden in the beginning. Satan would love nothing more than to get you running from your Father and moving toward achieving your own ends, toward getting revenge on the one who hurt you, toward isolation or self-destruction—anything but God's good plan for you.

Hannah went the other way. She brought all her sorrow, messy feelings, and pain straight to God. She in fact made a desperate plea:

> She made a vow, saying, "LORD Almighty, if you will only look on
> your servant's misery and remember me, and not forget your servant
> but give her a son, then I will give him to the LORD for all the days
> of his life, and no razor will ever be used on his head." (v. 11)

Later it says that after her prayer, even though no answer had come, she was able to eat again, and her mood was lifted.

If we read on a little in the chapter, we find out that Hannah got pregnant not only with Samuel but with more children thereafter. Not all stories end that way, though. Did her lifted mood mean Hannah trusted God's goodness, even if her prayer was never answered the way she hoped? Does that mean we can trust God too?

The "even if" statement is significant. It is poor theology to reduce God to a human level, saying he plays favorites, is good to some but not others, and is weighing everything on a big balance to see whether we are worthy of blessings. We can begin to let go of that fallible perspective of God. "Even if" means that no matter the outcome, we trust that God is still good.

Rich theology means a faith and hope that might shake you up a bit. If God is working all things for our good, then we might not even recognize the good in what is right in front of us. You might have to trust that what is good for her is not necessarily what is good for you. It doesn't mean God's rejection, despite what it might feel like.

Hannah was able to work out the real battle. She didn't confront or condemn her rival, whoever it was. On her knees before God, she was able to finally find relief. A relief that breathed, "Even if."

> *Rich theology means a faith and hope that might shake you up a bit.*

Not Another Platitude

Please hear me well: I don't mean to oversimplify this concept.

Those of us who have received (or offered) well-meaning but feeble attempts at advice know the refrains "Just go to God!" "Just pray about it!" "Just have faith!"

You might be familiar with the painful feelings that come from this advice. The assumption comes across that if you were simply a little more faithful, the blessing would come through. Or at least you wouldn't be hurting so much over it.

There is nothing simple about working out your heartbreak with your heavenly Father, no matter what the heartbreak looks like. Just as grief isn't one time only, surrender is ongoing, a practice of constantly working out the pain with him to find faith and hope through it all.

Although we only get to see this one desperate prayer moment with Hannah, I'm guessing it wasn't her first time crying out to God. We read the Scriptures and only see moments or days over what sometimes actually took months or years. We don't know how long Hannah struggled with infertility and was antagonized by her rival, and we don't know how many times she actually spoke with God about it.

As Proverbs 14:10 says, "Each heart knows its own bitterness, and no one else can fully share its joy" (NLT).

We as people can connect and relate to one another. We can pray for one another. We can counsel one another. I'm a huge advocate for therapy and having someone there to ask you the right questions and help point you back to the truth.

But there is only one who can fully understand, who knows us deeply and is significantly familiar with all our ways (see Ps. 139:3), the only one who hems us in behind and before (see v. 5). And that's our compassionate, generous, deeply loving Creator.

Just as people are not your biggest enemy, they are also not your biggest source of relief when it comes to heartbreak. Peace and surrender cannot be fully found by working out our pain with people. We can pray together, get advice, share, and relate. But people can't answer our biggest questions. People are not our Creator. If we cannot settle our deepest questions and disputes with him, how can we trust him in our lives moving forward? We can't.

Our peace comes from this: that the God who knows you by heart and has you engraved on the palm of his hand (see Isa. 49:16) invites you to work through the sorrows and challenges directly with him.

Just as grief isn't one time only, surrender is ongoing, a practice of constantly working out the pain with him to find faith and hope through it all.

Here's what I can tell you about the period of infertility I experienced: It was painful. It was scary. Not everyone understood. And yet it was a time in my life when God and I became closer than ever before. Not because he quickly and spontaneously granted me wisdom and clarity to take away my worry and pain, but because I simply needed him and had nowhere else to go. Every desperate and bewildered prayer. Every decision to show up when being there felt the hardest (even at baby showers). Every question met with biblical promises instead of how I was feeling at the time. Conversations with the people he put in my life who could relate. The ways God came through in this valley led to faith and confidence that grew more steady and less shakable over time.

Eventually I found myself staring down at a positive pregnancy test only a week before a surgery to figure out why I *couldn't* get pregnant. I ended up becoming a mom. As I write this, I have two children and my third on the way, but even now that season of life is not lost on me. The season when I didn't know if what I hoped for would ever happen. The season of working it out between God and me, and adopting the stance of "even if."

Sometimes our questions for God can drown out our cries of help to him. We run away from God instead of running to him because the real answer might not be the one we want.

When your questions feel too big and your problem too insignificant for God, remember that God is the God of good plans and good things for us. He orchestrates our lives for our greatest good—which might look different from our carefully mapped-out plans. Know that when you come to him, even with questions or tears or pain, he welcomes you in. He is here with you for the long haul, through every difficult moment and all kinds of emotions.

In the Meantime

At some point in every challenging season, while wrestling it all out with God, our consciousness starts to shift.

The pain and fear don't go away, but they become a little less consuming. At some point in the journey, we start feeling less disoriented and begin to focus on what we can see and do instead of what we can't.

During that stage of infertility, I continued to set up appointments with doctors who could help. And I also continued working my job and shepherding a ministry at church with my husband. Infertility wasn't the only season in which I kept busy. While struggling to start my career during my early marriage and postgrad days, I began a blog and served at church where I could. In the early days of the pandemic, I focused on keeping my kids engaged and making our home a comfortable and safe place to quarantine.

Why? Because the longer I felt stalled indefinitely in my pain, the more time I had to focus on it, nursing my wounds. My own pain would swell, leading to insecurity about God, jealousy, envy, competition, and bitterness. The rival started to win.

As you become familiar with the practice of continually surrendering your deepest griefs and desires to God, you might find yourself wondering what's next or what to do in the meantime. My encouragement to you is to have time and space to grieve and cry out to God if you need it, and also to not stop moving in your worship and purpose with God.

When you're stuck or stalled, here are some imperfect practices to try. The secret is this: they work best preventatively, implemented during a calmer season of life, instead of only being applied like a bandage to a tough time for a quick fix. And even in those moments, they might need to be put to use again and again. It's practice, not perfection.

1. Cultivate Gratitude

Studies show that a consistent gratitude practice over time will have a long-term return of greater happiness, lower depression, lower stress, greater connections with others, more generosity, and less motivation by guilt.[1]

But long before those studies were performed, the Bible prompted us to "rejoice in the Lord always.… Do not be anxious about anything, but in every situation, by prayer and petition, with thanksgiving, present your requests to God" (Phil. 4:4, 6) and to "rejoice always, pray continually, give thanks in all circumstances" (1 Thess. 5:16–18a). It also shows that Jesus often gave thanks, especially prior to the incredible miracles he performed. (Ann Voskamp drew my attention to this fact with her wonderful book *One Thousand Gifts*.)[2]

We as human beings don't tend to have giving thanks as our default. (Or maybe that's just me.) It comes more naturally to worry or see the negative instead of the positive. That's why the Scriptures remind us to give thanks and why it's not something you just flip on and off like a light switch.

The way to set yourself up for success in the challenging season is to set up a practice of gratitude in any season. Take a few minutes every day, maybe after you wake up or before bed, to think about or even write down things you're grateful for—as opposed to the immediate, problem-solving thinking that says, *It could be worse*, or *At least you ... aren't alone ... have your health ... still have a job ...* etc. This practice sets up a healthy mindset that gives you a solid foundation to stand on when the difficult news or season comes in.

2. Go Back to the Promises That Keep You Going

In my lowest moments, I felt stuck and stalled. I was waiting for the day my circumstances changed (and often felt discouraged until that happened). Somewhere in a down season, it occurred to me how much time was wasted in my waiting for things to be different.

Why does God have you where you are? Do you believe he is intentional in his plans and capable of change if it is his will? Do you believe that he is good and has your best in mind? If we believe in who God is and what he promises us, we can hardly stay stranded.

God's promises to us speak directly to our wounded, weary, and waiting spirits. Here are some of my favorites.

> **God has set up plans for us with purpose and intention:** "From one man he made all the nations, that they should inhabit the whole earth; and he marked out their appointed times in history and the boundaries of their lands. God did this so that they would seek him and perhaps reach out for him and find him, though he is not far from any one of us" (Acts 17:26–27).

> **God has made us capable and equipped to do his work:** "His divine power has given us everything we need for a godly life

through our knowledge of him who called us by his own glory and goodness" (2 Pet. 1:3).

God is always working for our good: "We know that in all things God works for the good of those who love him, who have been called according to his purpose" (Rom. 8:28).

The doubts that say we are the exception to God's great promises, that he favors others, that he doesn't have a plan for us, or that he wants to withhold good from us all fall apart when we go back to God's Word and hold tightly to it.

While our disappointments, discouragements, and despair are real and valid, they are not meant to have the final say in our lives, trapping us under false assumptions about our loving Father or those around us.

When you are in the middle of doubts and fears, keep going back to the assurances God provides for just those moments. Believe that there is more beyond the circumstances you can see. Know that he doesn't pit us against each other for any reason and that he is currently—yes, even right now—in the process of working out good for you and your life.

Let's Do This

Write down promises from God that help steady your faith in him when life feels painful and your doubts start rearing their ugly heads. Keep the promises handy by memorizing them, posting them on sticky notes throughout your home, or keeping them in a journal by your bed.

Work It Out

1. Think of a hope deferred that felt unbearable to you. What helped you get through it? What were some doubts you had to work through with God, and how did he show himself in it all?

2. What will your practice of surrender to God look like? Draw out a battle plan for moments that feel desperate or times when your rival won't stop provoking you.

3. What are some practical ways you can show up for other people even if they're going through a different season than you? Write down three ways you can celebrate a friend's joy and three ways you can support them in their waiting or disappointment.

Three truths I know about God

-
-

Three things I'm grateful for

-
-
-

Three steps I can take moving forward

-
-
-

Find the link on page 28.

Video Notes

Reflective Prayer

Prayer Requests

Praises

Chapter 3

The Woman Who Disagrees with You

If you and social media had existed in the days of the early churches, you might have seen some of the following show up in your newsfeed:

@corinthiandisciple: Just heard an amazing lesson from Paul in the synagogue!

@believer_est33: You follow Paul?!? Please please please come with me to hear Cephas preach instead—it'll blow you away!!

@saved4ever: If you ask me, Paul is waaay too liberal. I don't trust that Cephas either. Apollos baptized me, and I won't listen to anyone but him.

@holierthanthou: I can't believe what I'm reading. How can ANY of you call yourselves believers?! The only one I follow is CHRIST. You should be ashamed.

@septuagintscholar: Bro! Did I just see you tagged in a picture at a Gentile party?!

@keys2thekingdom: Don't know what you're talking about.

@apostlepaul: REALLY, Peter? In denial again?

@prosperousjourney: Please pray for me. Dealing with certain people who just don't know how to let things go. Also any advice on being patient in trying times??

@syntychesays: Way to be SUPER OBVIOUS, Euodia. If you have something to say, JUST SAY IT!!!!

Let's be honest. It probably wouldn't look all that different than it does today.

These are the days of keyboard warriors and social media showdowns. I'm guilty of grabbing hold of my laptop and fiercely attempting to crusade online for others or, more honestly, for my personal opinions. Maybe you can relate? Despite my good(?) intentions, I've neither succeeded in changing anyone's mind nor felt victorious when all was said and done. Just foolish.

The truth? Conflict existed long before the days of status updates and discussion boards. The argument could be made that we're handling it in a healthier way these days. At least we don't still practice the deadly duels or Old West showdowns of the past, right? And yet the divisions between us feel bigger and more obvious than ever before.

Was it always like this? So heated and hostile and polarized? Perhaps it was—or maybe we were just quieter about it.

Unfortunately, contrary to what Jesus asks us to do (love, invite, serve, and seek peace and unity), Christians usually seem to be at the center of heated debates, whether among ourselves or with those who have differing beliefs. One popular Christianese phrase today is "holding the line," meaning loudly and forcefully standing strong on your convictions, no matter what anyone says. This one in particular nags at me. Rather than referencing Scripture, it sounds more like creating ripples of division and hierarchy. When did Jesus ask us to do this? Are we meant to set up red tape of church approval the way we see fit, or to bring unity and hope to a broken world by pointing people to Jesus' incredible love?

But back to disagreements—they usually come from one (or multiple) of several different places:

- Dislike or hatred of individuals or groups
- Desire to establish superiority
- Pursuit of self-interest
- Difference of values, beliefs, or experience
- Straight-up misunderstanding or misinformation

We also handle conflict differently. Some go in ready for a fight. It can be a love language for you to speak your mind, work out your differences, and lay it all on the table. You have a hard time grasping the idea of passive aggressiveness or the silent treatment. Why not just deal with it?

Me? I find myself on the far end of the other extreme. Facing someone's wrath or reproach feels like torture and causes panic attacks. I hesitate to present a contrasting opinion, even if I disagree. Conflict feels fatal.

No matter how we approach it, whoever we are facing off with is not the enemy. Not even pesky online trolls or that one sister at church you're always at odds with or the family member that likes to stir up trouble. We don't need to fear being disagreeable, or even fear conflict itself.

God's goal for us is surprisingly not the complete absence of disagreement. Meanwhile, Satan's greatest aim is always to throw us into discord and division.

Shalom

When I heard the subject of the message that Sunday morning—*shalom*—I may have rolled my eyes a little.

Peace was an ongoing subject at church from 2020 onward, and rightly so. As a church, we were addressing topics like racism, gender roles, political divides, even disagreements based on the pandemic (such as "masks or no masks"). It was time to seek unity and not let our disagreements drive us apart.

But in my understanding, *shalom* translated to "peace," and I simply defined *peace* as "no conflict." Meaning, everyone in agreement, with zero fighting. The image that came to mind was a group of people holding hands in a circle around a campfire, wearing rose-colored glasses and singing songs about getting along. With how the social climate felt at the moment, this seemed like a far stretch. So while I was hopeful for peace, and I knew the Bible emphasized it, I feared an oversimplified sermon that would basically tell us to "just stop fighting and get along, okay?"

As the guest speaker worked his way through the message that day, though, my eyes widened, my heart softened, and my fingers started rapidly tapping eager notes on my phone. His first move was to completely redefine the word *shalom*. And by "redefine," I mean define it as it actually means, not the way I'd interpreted it all those years. It has a completely different meaning than the simple English definition we use for "peace": freedom from disturbance, tranquility, no war.

In his book *Shalom: The Bible's Word for Salvation, Justice and Peace*, Perry B. Yoder breaks down the meaning of *shalom* and its Greek counterpart, *eiréné* (*εἰρήνη*[1]), similarly to how the speaker did that day.[2]

According to Yoder, *shalom* means, in my my own understanding, a state of well-being where everything is as it should be: whole, flourishing, and all right for everyone involved. This applies in three specific ways: material and physical well-being, wellness and equality in relationships and society, and morality in the sense of integrity and honesty. Yoder emphasizes that *shalom* has a positive connotation: it's not so much about what it lacks (like conflict), but more about genuine welfare for everyone involved. This includes prosperity—not that everyone has surpassing wealth but that there is enough or more than enough to go around.[3]

Eiréné is used in the same contexts in the New Testament, but it also includes a theological meaning: that Jesus brings justification between people and God, and among human beings as well. It basically encompasses the good news of the gospel: unity and wholeness with God and others.[4]

Shalom is the thriving state of being that God intends for us. It involves all the aspects, not just one or two, and our shalom is interwoven with the shalom of those around us.

This beautiful definition brings so much more richness and abundance to a concept I thought I knew so well. What a mission! Not just to have everyone play nice with each other and cover up pesky disagreements but to work for the well-being of people made in the image of God.

> *Shalom is the thriving state of being that God intends for us.*

Yoder puts it this way: "*Shalom makers thus strive for total reconciliation*—among people, putting an end to want, oppression, and deception; and between people and God, so that all can live in the newness of life that is the vision of shalom."[5]

Another incredible interpretation of this concept and our mission is beautifully written by author Osheta Moore in her book *Shalom Sistas*: "Shalom is the breadth, depth, climate, and smell of the kingdom of God. It's a counter-story, with nothing missing and nothing lost for everyone who reads it. We become peacemakers when we, through the guidance of the Holy Spirit, catch glimpses of shalom and pull our friends to stand in our line of vision so that they too can see the beauty of the kingdom."[6]

That was certainly a far cry from my former view of peace. This is God's true business of shalom—the business we need to make our own.

The Opposite of Shalom

If true shalom is God's ultimate goal for his creation, then you can bet Satan opposes it.

Where God wants us whole, Satan wants us broken. Where God seeks a community that practices justice, unity, and equality, Satan seeks injustice, oppression, and division. Where God pursues our well-being, Satan pursues our destruction.

His top target? The church. The ruler of this world can break the world, no problem. He's done it many times: slavery, genocide, war, violence, injustice, abuse. But if he can infiltrate the church and have us tear each other apart? As we reflect God poorly in the process? That's his version of success. Why would people want to be part of a kingdom that looks just like the world? And worse, hypocritically pretends that it doesn't? What hope and wholeness would seekers find there?

We can even demand peace (e.g., no arguing) while dismissing the very real pain and harm some are experiencing. Yoder cautions strongly against this in his book.[7] It goes against the very definition of *shalom* for some to enjoy prosperity while others suffer. Sadly, I've been part of perpetuating this in the church—wanting to keep the status quo and avoid people being angry with each other, trying to "keep the peace." How eye opening it was to start really listening to brothers and sisters who experience oppression, especially based on their race. This is why knowing the true meaning of *shalom* as God intended makes a huge difference in the kind of peace we pursue. Satan would love for us to be divided by our pain and allow parts of our community, our brothers and sisters, to suffer in silence.

Where God pursues our well-being, Satan pursues our destruction.

When it comes to individual conflict, your Enemy wants you to bite your tongue. In the interest of my former definition of peace, he wants you to not rock the boat or make waves, often at the expense of your own heart, as bitterness and ambivalence grow.

Or he would prefer for you to get angry and say and do things you will later regret, things that cause more brokenness than wellness in the relationships in your life. And when that happens, he'd encourage you to fake repentance for the sake of "getting along" or to continue to stay divided and angry.

How do we battle the Devil's schemes in the very body of Christ and, on a larger scale, in the world? How do we keep worldliness from creeping in, causing cracks that lead to breaks? How do we intentionally work toward shalom for all people in this world, even if we disagree along the way?

Practical Pursuit of Shalom

Paul was familiar with working out conflict in the early days of the church. (Those newsfeed examples from the beginning of the chapter are all based on real conflicts he called out in his letters.) He wrote two passages in particular that seem to parallel each other when it comes to establishing peace and unity: Ephesians 4 and Colossians 3. Let's look at these verses and pull some helpful pointers and practical tips from them in our pursuit of shalom.

1. Put on Your New Self

You're not the person you used to be. Colossians 3:1–4 reminds us that while we used to be dead (in our sin, according to Ephesians 2), we've been raised with Christ, completely new.

Ephesians 4 takes it a step further, saying in verses 22–24: "You were taught, with regard to your former way of life, to put off your old self, which is being corrupted by its deceitful desires; to be made new in the attitude of your minds; and to put on the new self, created to be like God in true righteousness and holiness." (Colossians 3:9–10 also talks about being renewed to be more like God.)

Not only are we called to peace, unity, and wholeness, but we are *more than equipped* by God to live this out. We have been transformed and continue to be transformed. Our job is to keep putting off that old self that threatens to get in the way again—the old self that diminished others' well-being and prioritized our own, was blissful in its ignorance, relied solely on its own experience, and gave in to hatred. We instead keep renewing our minds, staying soft and open to God shaping us to be more like him.

Remember, our issues with other people aren't just relational issues. Everything we do stems from our identity: who God says we are. We can't really approach other practical tips until we have our identity down. And your identity is one made new.

Everything we do stems from our identity: who God says we are.

2. Seek to Be One with God's People

The divisions that might have kept us apart in our old lives do not mean anything now that we have been made new.

Ephesians 4:4–6 describes it like this: "There is one body and one Spirit, just as you were called to one hope when you were called; one Lord, one faith, one baptism; one God and Father of all, who is over all and through all and in all."

Similarly, Colossians 3:11 specifies, "Here there is no Gentile or Jew, circumcised or uncircumcised, barbarian, Scythian, slave or free, but Christ is all, and is in all." Verse 15 says, "Let the peace of Christ rule in your hearts, since as members of *one body* you were called to peace."

Paul didn't shy away from calling out the divisions we create for ourselves in society, specifically naming groups that wouldn't have had anything to do with each other at the time. He effectively says we don't have any excuse in the kingdom of God. Those who claim Christ are our brothers and sisters. We are one. And as one, we look out for each other.

Even those who do not claim Christ are those you are pointing to Christ. So is it okay to treat them differently (or indifferently)? Not so long as we are made new. (See point 1.)

3. Get Rid of Earthly Characteristics

Part of putting off our old selves is getting rid of the things that get in the way of our being transformed. Paul calls us to take drastic action:

> Put to death, therefore, whatever belongs to your earthly nature: sexual immorality, impurity, lust, evil desires and greed, which is idolatry. Because of these, the wrath of God is coming. You used to walk in these ways, in the life you once lived. But now you must

also rid yourselves of all such things as these: anger, rage, malice, slander, and filthy language from your lips. Do not lie to each other, since you have taken off your old self with its practices. (Col. 3:5–9)

In Ephesians 4:31, Paul encourages, "Get rid of all bitterness, rage and anger, brawling and slander, along with every form of malice." Earlier on, he warns us that a life without God leads to a hardened heart, ignorance, and a giving of ourselves over to sensuality and greed (vv. 18–19). I can relate to these steps, and I bet you can too. The times I give in to sin usually come when I'm ignoring what God prompts my heart to do and I choose what I want to do instead.

It's a process, and not a perfect one, but God doesn't expect it to be. We learn by staying engaged with God. Remove sin, or opportunities to sin, from the equation. Come up with a plan for what to do when your sinful nature intervenes, and continue to practice it.

We have to do this with anger in our family, both parents and kids. We all have had to sit down and, after necessary apologies, come up with ways that are and aren't appropriate for dealing with our angry feelings. (Appropriate: taking a break, counting to ten, exercising or moving in a way that isn't violent or destructive. Not appropriate: yelling, saying hurtful things, throwing or kicking things. All of which I've done and had to apologize for, by the way.)

4. Put on Godly Characteristics

When you remove something, you don't leave the space empty, with plenty of room for what you removed to return. You replace it with something else. In this case, we remove the earthly and replace it with the godly.

Paul breaks down a godly character for us in Galatians 5:22–23: "The fruit of the Spirit is love, joy, peace, forbearance, kindness, goodness, faithfulness, gentleness and self-control. Against such things there is no law."

Peter gives us his own list in 2 Peter 1:5–7: "Make every effort to add to your faith goodness; and to goodness, knowledge; and to knowledge, self-control; and to self-control, perseverance; and to perseverance, godliness; and to godliness, mutual affection; and to mutual affection, love."

There's no confusion here. These verses assume that we ourselves and others are imperfect, possibly even (say it isn't so!) doing things that require forbearance or forgiveness. We're human. We make mistakes. We are also growing in these fruits of the Spirit and disciplines.

5. Speak What Is True and Helpful

We don't need to be silent.

And all the conflict warriors breathed a sigh of relief! The conflict avoiders? Not so much. Either way, stay with me.

First, let's go back to our identities in God, through Christ. We are made new. Our own self-interest is not the priority anymore. The things that may have divided us are no longer applicable. We are one! And we are equipped to work toward shalom.

Ephesians 4 says, "Each of you must put off falsehood and speak truthfully to your neighbor, for we are all members of one body" (v. 25), as well as this: "Do not let any unwholesome talk come out of your mouths, but only what is helpful for building others up according to their needs, that it may benefit those who listen" (v. 29).

Colossians 3:16–17 presents this beautiful picture that combines the two: "Let the message of Christ dwell among you richly as you teach and admonish one another with all wisdom through psalms, hymns, and songs from the Spirit, singing to God with gratitude in your hearts. And whatever you do, whether in word or deed, do it all in the name of the Lord Jesus, giving thanks to God the Father through him."

This tells us several things: That honesty, teaching, and admonishment have a place. That they are combined with gratitude and what is helpful. And that our words should be flowing with songs and Scripture.

Years ago, I attended a marriage retreat where the speakers unintentionally commended themselves not just for their years of marriage and strong relationship but also for the striking fact that whenever they spoke, they seemed to pour out Scripture. It was like their main language. I was more convicted by that than anything else I heard that weekend.

Here's the encouraging thing: we have access to every bit of wisdom we could possibly need.

> The law of the LORD is perfect,
>   refreshing the soul.
> The statutes of the LORD are trustworthy,
>   making wise the simple.
> The precepts of the LORD are right,
>   giving joy to the heart.
> The commands of the LORD are radiant,
>   giving light to the eyes.
> The fear of the LORD is pure,
>   enduring forever.
> The decrees of the LORD are firm,
>   and all of them are righteous. (Ps. 19:7–9)

As those who have been made new in Christ, we have the Holy Spirit within us, the Spirit that prompts us toward truth and stirs us when something doesn't seem quite right. Thankfully, we don't have to rely on our own wisdom to figure it all out or say the right thing—we have God's Word available to us anytime.

Also, it never hurts to approach others with humility. Maybe you're stirred toward something that actually needs to be revealed for you more than for the other person.

Disagreements versus Quarrels

Even though God and the church aren't threatened when we disagree, we can still contribute to brokenness in the body and miss the whole point by focusing on quarrels and quibbles over things that don't matter.

We waste time quarreling because of things like:

- Controversy, genealogies, and the law (Titus 3:9–11)
- Disputable matters (Rom. 14:1)
- Hot tempers (Prov. 15:18)
- Words (2 Tim. 2:14)
- What we desire or covet, or our own greed (James 4:1–2)
- Quarrelsome or nagging (Prov. 21:19)
- Self-righteousness (1 Cor. 1:10–12)
- Feeling offended (Prov. 19:11)
- Airing our opinions without seeking to understand (Prov. 18:1–2)

Scriptures cite our quarrels over questionable topics as a sign of our lack of self-control. So which is it? A quarrel from a lack of self-control? Or a disagreement worth addressing?

These questions are helpful for me to consider before speaking:

1. Have I been quick to listen, slow to speak, and slow to become angry in this situation, as James 1:19 says?
2. Have I taken time (even just a moment) to think and pray over this situation and this person before I say something? (If not, can I go back later and talk to her about it?)
3. What am I hoping will come out of this conversation?

4. What details do I need to ask for so that I can be clear in my understanding?

5. Is this the best context for this conversation? (e.g., Should we take it offline? Talk on the phone or in person? Bring a trusted friend along?)

6. Is this an area where we can agree to disagree?

7. Have I worked out peace as far as it depends on me? (Rom. 12:18)

Process and Practice

Working through conflict is just not something we are always going to get right. But as we work through our own valid feelings, personal experience, and sinful nature, even if we don't do things the best way, good can result from being willing to engage in disagreements.

Orville and Wilbur Wright, the brothers famous for making pioneering strides in aviation, were also known for their arguments, prompted from a young age by a father who encouraged them to participate in debates with each other. In one of his personal letters, Orville noted:

> No truth is without some mixture of error, and no error so false but that it possesses no element of truth. If a man is in too big a hurry to give up an error, he is liable to give up some truth with it, and in accepting the arguments of the other man he is sure to get some errors with it. Honest argument is merely a process of mutually picking the beams and motes out of each other's eyes so both can see clearly ...[8]

I wonder if he was consciously or unconsciously making a connection to Matthew 7:4–5: "How can you say to your brother, 'Let me take the speck out of your eye,' when all the time there is a plank in your own eye? You hypocrite, first take the plank out of your own eye, and then you will see clearly to remove the speck from your brother's eye."

The Wright brothers show us that we help each other find truth, even personal truth, by engaging in disagreements. We can trust when the Holy Spirit puts something on our hearts to say. And Matthew 7 reminds us to do this with grace and humility, because not a single one of us is perfect.

As we work our way through disagreements, let us remain rooted in our identities in God, seek shalom for everyone involved, speak what is truthful and helpful, and be both confident in how God is moving and humble in our own humanity.

Let's Do This

Spend some time thinking about an earthly characteristic you would like to "put to death" in your life and a godly characteristic you would like to replace it with. In the space below, create a battle plan for how you will counter the first and grow in the second this week, and be sure to include prayer in your plan.

Work It Out

1. How do you react in a moment of conflict with the woman who feels like the enemy? Would you say you go all in, or do you avoid it? What in this chapter helps you find neutral ground in how you respond to conflict?

_____

_____

_____

_____

_____

_____

_____

_____

_____

_____

_____

_____

_____

_____

_____

_____

_____

_____

_____

_____

2. What strikes you about the concept of shalom? How can it shape your response to someone in conflict with you?

3. Which of the practical tips in our pursuit of shalom (based on Ephesians 4 and Colossians 3) speaks the most to you? How can you apply it to how you approach conflict?

Three truths I know about God

- ✦
- ✦
- ✦

Three things I'm grateful for

- ✦
- ✦
- ✦

Three steps I can take moving forward

- ✦
- ✦
- ✦

Watch Video 3

Find the link on page 28.

Video Notes

Reflective Prayer

Prayer Requests

Praises

Chapter 4

The Woman Whose Suffering Scares You

Empty. Bitter. Afflicted.

In the book of Ruth, we come to know a broken and grieving woman named Naomi.[1] Just as we are introduced to her, death strikes her family not once, not twice, but three times. The devastating loss of her husband was followed by both of the grown sons she'd raised. Deep in sorrow, Naomi was tallying up last words and memories, wrestling with unanswerable questions, and struggling to get up in the morning.

Without her family, this woman's identity was shattered. In a patriarchal society in which only men held power and property, her security and provision were no longer guaranteed. (*How would she eat? Where would she live?*) The long-time roles she'd held as wife and mother had abruptly ended. (*What could she have done differently to hold on to her family longer?*) The vision of growing old with her husband, surrounded by her sons and grandchildren, had evaporated like mist. (*What did she have to look forward to now?*) Her home community was miles away, at least a week's journey by foot through rugged mountains. (*Would they even welcome her back?*) Her very faith was hanging by a thread, possibly beyond repair, at odds with the God who had formerly made her life match the meaning of her name, Naomi, which means "pleasant." (*Why had he now turned his back on her?*)

So when she used those three words—*empty, bitter, afflicted*—to describe her life after returning home to be with her people, the Israelites, all she got was silence. That was the response from her old friends and her community, because no one was in a place to disagree with her.

These days, someone might have said,

> *Maybe God has a lesson in this somewhere.*
> *Everything happens for a reason.*
> *At least you have your … (health, other family, home).*
> *You just need to have faith.*

I've said similar words, and I regret them. I've heard similar words and felt the sting of shame.

The sorrow we intuitively feel for those who are hurting comes as a result of being *imago dei*, image bearers of God. We want to make it better, to fix, to find reason, and to restore hope. Our hearts beat fast with distress and good intentions. *Life wasn't meant to be this way. Let's find a solution.*

As much as we want to help, the simple fact is, we feel, and we fear. Human instincts make us cringe and hold back. Misfortune feels uncomfortable, inconvenient, and contagious. We feel the need to distance ourselves far from it. In our well-meaning attempts to fix, we may rush past the problem, sweeping aside the pain. Or possibly, our own judgments of the situation get in the way of our love-in-action for those involved.

Let us put the Enemy in his place by learning how to love the way God does.

Again, Proverbs 14:10 says, "Each heart knows its own bitterness, and no one else can share its joy." The emotions of the heart can feel lonely, and loss feels devastating in ways we can't always express. What are we meant to do when others go through pain that we may not be able to comprehend? What does God want us to do?

In this journey, as we look to cultivate compassion rather than squelching it, we are fortunately not without hope or resources. We have the Word of God, the living and active answer to the questions we face as we attempt to live for God's glory in this world. We have the "divine power" that gives us "everything we need for a godly life through our knowledge of him who called us by his own glory and goodness" (2 Pet. 1:3). And I'm pretty sure that because Jesus knew this would be a struggle for us, he left us with many exhortations and examples of how to live this out practically and personally.

Your Enemy would rather have you recoil from discomfort and leave others isolated in their pain. Or in the opposite role: feeling neglected and alone where others fear to tread. He'd like you to believe the lie that no one cares and no one can help. This includes God—painting a picture of one who is too distant or disconnected to care about the very real heartbreak we experience.

Let us put the Enemy in his place by learning how to love the way God does.

Unfailing Compassion

Three words are typically used to describe how we relate to someone else's pain: *sympathy*, *empathy*, and *compassion*.[2] Sometimes we use them interchangeably, but they actually have three different meanings:

Sympathy says, "That makes sense." You understand why someone is going through something difficult, even if you haven't experienced the same thing.

Empathy says, "I feel with you." Romans 12:15 describes empathy well: "Rejoice with those who rejoice; mourn with those who mourn." Empathy involves feeling along with the person going through pain, perhaps literally, as when you see someone twist their ankle and your mirror neurons fire, making you feel sensitivity in the same spot. Or it means mentally putting yourself in that person's position to imagine what you would feel if it happened to you.

Compassion is a whole different [he]art form. It's not just emotional but relational—an ongoing practice of living in tune with those around you rather than in self-imposed isolation. Like the above traits, it's a choice to engage with others that involves emotion and action, but unlike sympathy and empathy, it's not simply a response to seeing someone in pain. It's developing the habit of noticing, engaging, walking alongside, and reaching out. Compassion is to look someone in the eyes and really see them. With eyes opened by compassion, we have an awareness that finds the full picture, not just the present circumstances. (For example, realizing there is much more to someone than a bad day, cranky expression, angry words, or poor choices.)

Compassion literally means "to suffer with,"[3] to stick around in the pain, and stay present in it. There is a definite physical element to it: the Bible sometimes translates it as being "deeply stirred."[4] Today, we might use the words *heartbreaking*, *gut-wrenching*, or *spine-tingling* when it comes to feeling someone else's pain—it affects us at our core, in a physical way. With this kind of cultivated heart, choosing to know others deeply, we are prompted to act.

Compassion says, "I am completely moved. I am here in the suffering with you. What can I do?"

Out of all the words to describe the one and only Alpha and Omega, what's one of the most used? *Compassionate.* The New International Version contains eighty-one verses with the word *compassion*, and all but nine refer to God or Jesus or are related to them. (For example, our compassion being a result of our relationship to God.) He is "the Father of compassion and the God of all comfort," according to 2 Corinthians 1:3–4. It's the first word he uses to describe himself in Exodus 34:6, as he passes before Moses: "The LORD, the LORD, the compassionate and gracious God, slow to anger, abounding in love and faithfulness …"

Parallel with the description of God's compassion, these verses show us other aspects of his character: kind, gracious, abundantly loving, providing, comforting. Compassion is described as an eager and active kind of love: "The LORD longs to be gracious to you," Isaiah 30:18 says, "therefore he will rise up to show you compassion."

The King of Kings, sovereign over all creation, actually gets down on bended knee to look us in the eye and see us completely. And he even took it a step further: although he is holy and separate from us, he gave up his glory and his rights to come down and experience life as we do, embodied in Jesus Christ.

What Jesus encountered while living among us broke him: the physical and mental illness, our disconnection with God, the barriers to our relationship with him, our shame, death. In those moments, Jesus wept, cried out, felt frustrated and indignant, reached out and touched, healed, ate with, and went out of his way for people when he saw all these things firsthand. He was the very nature of God lived out so we could see it and feel it.

In the middle of all these descriptions of God's incredible compassion, God does something so unbelievable and yet relatable to us: he grapples. Some of these verses show God struggling with his compassion, or the writer fighting to find God's compassion in the middle of their challenges. God is both–and. He is both compassionate *and* feels anger; he is both gracious *and* absolutely just.

This thought brings an unexpected sense of comfort for me. Because we too grapple. We struggle. We have real feelings as we strive to live out compassion and relate to other people. Of course, God grapples out of his righteousness while we, on the other hand, grapple with our human natures. And yet we have a perfect example of a God whose compassion wins every time. "Because of the LORD's great love we are not consumed, for his compassions never fail. They are new every morning; great is your faithfulness" (Lam. 3:22–23).

The Deepest Kind of Love

As I lay on a long stretch of tissue paper that crinkled at every turn, a technician firmly maneuvered a handheld machine on the warm gel spread over my abdomen. I stared up at a screen and saw blobs in motion until shapes started to take form.

My eyes widened as I took in the sight of a pulsing heart separated into four chambers, of arms and legs wiggling at random. The technician marked off five tiny fingers as I silently made my own count, just to be sure. A small profile provided a two-dimensional view that was barely a glimpse of what my baby girl would look like, and it was all I had until she arrived.

But that was her. That was my daughter. I was head over heels for a being I only knew through belly flutters and a silhouette. Just as I was with her two brothers before her, who'd made their appearances on similar screens years earlier.

It might sound silly to deeply love someone you don't know, can barely see, and who happens to leave you sick, uncomfortable, and constantly tired as she grows through nutrients and oxygen you have to provide. And yet it's the most natural thing in the world. You two are intimately connected in a way you'll never quite be with anyone else.

The Hebrew word *rachum* (pronounced rakh-oom') means "compassionate"[5] and, as said before, is used in Scripture for the most part to describe God. Here's the thing: it shares a root with *rechem* (pronounced rekh'-em), meaning "womb."[6] Meaning that deeply intimate, tenderly nurturing, strongly protective, mysterious place where a baby grows. It is an innermost part that is unique to women.

Our God is near, active, engaged, deeply invested, intuitively motivated, and dearly loving toward us.

Elizabeth Barrett Browning wrote the sonnet beginning, "How do I love thee? Let me count the ways." In his own living personal sonnet to us, God starts with this: in the deepest, innermost part of himself, he holds the purest compassion, care, and abounding love for us. It's the same kind of love a mother (or father) feels for a child—this instinctive, automatic, committed, moving, motivating love that is intimate, fierce, strong, and not easily broken. There is something especially significant about a mother's intuitive love for the baby she grows and carries and is connected with in a way she'll never be connected with another, even another of her own children.

This kind of love may have been how you could describe your relationship with your parents. It may not. It may have been broken, sorely lacking, cut short, or unavailable. If that was your experience, I pray that you find hope and overwhelming love in this promise: that everything you wish you could have had, everything that fell short in that most core of relationships, can be found in God's patient, constant, faithful love for you.

> Can a mother forget the baby at her breast
>   and have no compassion on the child she has borne?
> Though she may forget,
>   I will not forget you!
> See, I have engraved you on the palms of my hands;
>   your walls are ever before me. (Isa. 49:15–16)

These words are specifically addressed to Zion, the nation of Israel. But they reflect God's heart for all his people. All of us. You are engraved right in the grip of his hand. Yes, you. God could open up his hands and point and say, "See? Right there."

Compassion always leaves an impact. It is mutual between both of the people involved and leaves neither untouched. Seeing God's love for us as deeply interconnected and compassionate, like a mother's love, melts me. God sees me as I see my children: with all the hopes, dreams, and possibilities before them. With all the love I have for them, simply knowing they are mine. With the delight that comes from watching them grow, celebrating their victories, craving the best intentions for them. With an ache for them when they hurt or make the wrong choices.

Our God is near, active, engaged, deeply invested, intuitively motivated, and dearly loving toward us. We need never fear that we can fumble and break our relationship with him or that he won't forgive us. His compassions truly never fail.

Compassion Embodied

One day in Galilee, a man approached Jesus who had no business being anywhere near him. The man had a highly contagious skin disease, identified in some translations as leprosy. According to the Jewish law, he should have sheepishly announced his presence by calling, "Unclean! Unclean!" Not that he could have hidden his disease. The book of Luke says he was "covered with leprosy" (5:12) which means it wasn't just on a small patch of his skin. Everyone in the community probably knew who he was and did their best to stay away from him.

This man's actions and words indicated that he believed Jesus held a power no one else did. He begged on his knees, saying, "If you are willing, you can make me clean" (Mark 1:40).

And how did Jesus respond? Did he react with disgust? "Get away from me! You're contagious! I can't get leprosy right now! Don't you know I have work to do!?" *Not a chance!*

Maybe he added the tormented man to his busy schedule, distancing himself until he could squeeze him in at some point in the near future: "Whoa there, pal! Submit something in writing, and I can get back to you in three to five business days, okay?" *Not in any version!*

Verse 41 tells us, "Jesus was indignant. He reached out his hand and touched the man. 'I am willing,' he said. 'Be clean!'"

Most English translations, however, start this way: "Moved with compassion, Jesus ..." The Greek actually uses a word that means "having been moved with compassion."[7] The New International Version uses *indignant*. The definition for *indignant* is "feeling or showing anger because of something unjust or unworthy," according to *Merriam-Webster Dictionary*.[8] Some take this to mean that Jesus was irritated that the man said, "If you are willing," as though his faith wasn't strong enough.

I can't speak for Jesus, but that theory about him doesn't sit well with me. Maybe, instead, Jesus was compassionately indignant? Perhaps he was disturbed in his soul about the years of agony this man had suffered, not only physically but mentally and emotionally as well. Imagine the isolation the leper endured and the pain of being "unclean." And then there was the barrier from the temple. (Those who were unclean were not permitted to enter.) Remember, God cares about our shalom—our wholeness and well-being. *Life wasn't meant to be that way. Absolutely not. Let's find a solution.*

So Jesus did the unthinkable: he reached out to touch the man. The people of the time and culture naturally would have assumed that through a single touch, Jesus made himself unclean. But instead of the man's "uncleanness" being passed on to Jesus, something miraculous happened: Jesus' clean was enough for the both of them. The man became healed, whole again, and clean—both physically and spiritually.

Jesus did the unthinkable: he reached out to touch the man.

God's particular brand of compassion is nearly incomprehensible to us. It goes beyond what is expected. There are other examples of Jesus healing people when he simply says the word and the person is healed. He doesn't even need to be in the same place. If he was truly irritated over the man's lack of faith, perhaps he would have done it that way. Yet a moved-with-compassion Jesus felt deeply for this man, who probably hadn't come in contact with another human being for a long time. Jesus reached out. He touched.

What Compassion Looks Like

Back to the story of Naomi. Two women in her life had compassion that also rose above what was expected.

Naomi's two sons had been married, so of course their wives were left in a situation similar to Naomi's. These women, Orpah and Ruth, were young though, and they had their communities around them, so they had a chance to start again. Yet when Naomi planned a return to her people in Israel, they packed up and started the journey with her. Naomi only allowed them to be so generous before she turned around and sent them home. "Thanks for being so kind to me. But you'll have better luck here among your people. I don't have anything else to offer you," she essentially says in the first chapter of Ruth.

Both of them, again, did what anyone would: they cried and offered one last time to go with her. Again, she dissuaded them. So Orpah turned and headed home.

We sometimes paint Orpah to be the "bad guy" in this story, as though she were the disloyal, unfaithful one. But think about it: Truly, she did a lot for her grieving mother-in-law. She had packed up and was willing to live among a new community in a new country. That sounds like a lot to me, and possibly more than was called for in her culture. I wonder if her people scrutinized her decision.

Meanwhile, Naomi called it an act of kindness and told her it would be better if she stayed with her own family.

Sometimes our "beyond what is expected" doesn't match what someone else can do. That's okay. Depending on your stage of life and circumstances, maybe packing up or going part of the way is all you can do for someone, and that is enough. Orpah doesn't deserve our judgment or an unfair comparison to Ruth. They're not in opposition.

Ruth did go with Naomi, flatly refusing to turn back. And here it seems to go back to that original definition of *compassion*: "to struggle with." That too is the kind of love that God displays for us: unexpected, above and beyond. This decision, along with her faith and obedience, changed the course of Ruth's life (not to mention Naomi's) and happened to place her squarely in the genealogy of Jesus.

Who knows what God has planned for us and others when compassion shapes our mindset and actions?

The famed children's TV show host Fred Rogers is one of my heroes, by virtue of his compassion, conviction, and character. He exemplified compassion in many ways, mostly unassuming ones that still managed to leave a giant impact for everyone in his "neighborhood," on-screen and off. One of his most famous quotes goes like this: "Love isn't a state of perfect caring. It is an active noun like *struggle*. To love someone is to strive to accept that person exactly the way he or she is, right here and now."[9]

It's particularly poignant that he uses *struggle* as the example of the verb. Compassion and love are choices. They're as active as the struggle someone else is going through. You might even say that compassion is the opposing force for whatever someone is enduring and battling at the time. Sometimes we're the ones who can offer to compassionately struggle with; sometimes we're the ones right in the middle of the struggle.

"Carry each other's burdens," says Paul in Galatians 6:2, "and in this way you will fulfill the law of Christ." This is the way we can do it: through compassion.

Heart with Ears

God's timing is mysterious and predictably unpredictable. Right around the time I started working on this chapter, we received the news that my mother-in-law was dying. There was something incredibly poignant about having to navigate this particular chapter as it coincided with the dark season we found ourselves in.

Like Naomi, my mother-in-law was a woman worthy of loyalty to the ends of the earth. Her son grew up to be a testimony to her example in his life: responsible, steady, strong, funny, generous, fiercely devoted to family, and honorable. Her family was her world, and she was head over heels for her grandchildren. There really are no words to express the absence she leaves behind in our lives.

> Who knows what God has planned for us and others when compassion shapes our mindset and actions?

When you don't know how to respond, you talk to the people who do. My sister-in-law, Allie, is a grief counselor, and I reached out to her for help in how to approach all of this, both grieving and being there for the one in grief.

"My best advice for you," she said, referencing her training with the Grief Recovery Institute, "is to be a heart with ears."[10] Her summary of the concept was this: when others are in pain, it's not our time to fix or adjust but to hear. To be with. To feel with. To sit in the struggle with.

So what can we do when it comes to compassionate living?

- Cultivate compassion by being aware and engaged with those around you.
- Look people in the eyes.
- Do more than what is expected.
- Be a heart with ears.
- Help carry each other's burdens.

In this way, you will fulfill the law of Christ and grow more in the character of our Creator.

Let's Do This

Watch the video "Where Does Compassion Come From?" by Twill on YouTube (special thanks to my friend TR who sent me this): www.youtube.com/watch?v=A4a66aFalME.

Then consider the people you interact with on an average day with whom you might not completely engage. (The person at the cash register? The person behind the desk? A coworker?) Write their name and a way you can make it a point to really see and engage with them.

Work It Out

1. The first word God used to describe himself in Exodus 34:6 is *compassionate*. Why do you think this is such a core part of his identity? What does that mean for us?

2. Mark 1:41 shows us that Jesus was "indignant" or "moved to compassion." What would it look like to be indignant or moved to compassion on behalf of someone else and their suffering, instead of scared or angered by it?

3. Compassion is how we help carry each other's burdens and often goes beyond what is expected by society. Think about an example of this in your own life. How did someone show you compassion beyond what was expected?

Three truths I know about God

✦

✦

✦

Three things I'm grateful for

✦

✦

✦

Three steps I can take moving forward

✦

✦

✦

Watch Video 4

Find the link on page 28.

Video Notes

Reflective Prayer

Prayer Requests

Praises

Chapter 5

The Woman Who Doesn't Believe

Remember that girl from chapter 1 who tried to make herself invisible?

Well, there was one day in particular, in the high stakes world of middle school, in which that plan failed spectacularly.

Although I made Jesus Lord of my life at a young age and knew that one of our goals was to spread the good news, I was super uncomfortable about sharing my faith. It's not surprising, given how socially anxious and insecure I was, not to mention (*hello!*) it was the beginning of my teen years. That particular season of awkwardness is something I think I can safely say that we all experience.

But my desire to please God sometimes pushed me out of my comfort zone. Over the summer, I had been convicted by a lesson about not being ashamed of God, and the speaker challenged us to do something bold, like bring our Bibles with us to school.

So on the first day of eighth grade, I put on my brand-new outfit, packed up my L.L.Bean backpack with a lunch bag and new folders, and after a moment's debate, added my Teen Study Bible.

The minute we got our lockers, I stealthily looked around me and, smooth as a secret agent, slipped the Bible onto a shelf, then shut the door quickly. Mission accomplished. Our class returned to our homeroom.

Ten minutes later, the classroom intercom buzzed to life. A secretary addressed our teacher: "We've had a bit of a mix-up with the lockers. We'll need your class to come up and switch."

Pause.

"Also ... is there a *Jenn* in your class?" I blushed bright red and raised my hand. Upon the teacher's confirmation, the administrative assistant responded with, "Well, we're *especially* proud of Jenn." *Oh, dear.*

It turned out that the same set of lockers had been assigned to two classes. While the administration was trying to figure out which class occupied that set of lockers, they'd had to break into one. Can you guess whose locker they broke into?

The administrative assistant practically glowed as she made no small deal of the "mature" eighth grader who'd brought her Bible to school. I have no doubt she told several teachers and staff, overheard by more students. Meanwhile, I continued to blush. *Well played, God.*

We can all laugh about it together—my attempts to covertly comply with a spiritual challenge to appease my conscience in the least uncomfortable way possible. And how God, in his infinite wisdom and keen sense of humor, didn't let me off the hook quite so easily.

Let's just say that making God known is a mission that far surpasses the awkward and uncomfortable situation I made it out to be. But out of our own insecurity, we make the other woman the enemy—the one who will inflict judgment, ask too many questions, humiliate or misunderstand us. We become afraid, frustrated, and perhaps even judgmental of these women instead of loving them and seeing them as fellow image bearers. Yet the more we dig in, the more we realize that only the real Enemy is keeping us on the offensive, not each other.

The Inconsistency

Maybe as you read through my silly story, you took note of the glaring inconsistency: The whole point was to be unashamed of God, right? Instead, I ended up hiding and embarrassed at the "exposure."

It was the same with asking friends to come to teen ministry events or inviting other campus students to Bible discussions. I did it awkwardly and hesitantly and only because it was the "right thing to do." My own self-righteousness and reputation were the goal. The biggest issue wasn't sharing my faith or pointing people to Christ; it was proving my status as a "good Christian" by checking a challenge off a to-do list.

My weak efforts all had to do with my theology, which admittedly was rather mixed up at the time. You see, when I came out of the waters of baptism several months before that fateful first day of eighth grade, in my understanding, I was both saved *and* completely responsible for my own salvation going forward. It was like Jesus had cleared my slate of all past sin and now I had better keep that slate clean to earn my place with God.

When earning is the mindset, grace becomes very small. Shame plays a much bigger role. Instead of getting familiar with an abundance of grace that saves completely and helping others to find it, fear and self-protection win out. *What if you aren't good enough for God? What if everyone else finds out what a mess you really are?*

In all my concern over my own salvation, sharing with others felt intimidating. I feared bringing them into the stress and shame I myself felt. Why share about a faith that brings freedom and peace when they seemed nowhere to be found?

This false theology started to undo me. Years and years later, I broke down with anxiety attacks, realizing I couldn't keep it all together. I always felt like I was disappointing God. I hid behind the "good Christian" mask and checked the boxes, yet I avoided conflict and vulnerability and relationships and challenges because I was too afraid to be revealed for the mess I really was.

The Invitation

But God, in his limitless patience and grace, intervened and sent the right people at the right time, ones that could point me back to Scripture and make me aware of what Jesus really said and lived out. God's real purpose and promises for us go so far beyond what my narrow perspective was at the time.

In case you're anything like I was, let me tell you something you may not realize: God is not frustrated with your shortcomings or weighing your worth and lovability on a scale. There is no tally system. As the lyrics of "Jireh" by Elevation Worship and Maverick City Music go,

> *I'll never be more loved than I am right now*
> *Wasn't holding You up so there's nothing I can do to let You down*
> *Doesn't take a trophy to make You proud*
> *I'll never be more loved than I am right now.*[1]

It is also not God's goal to make you the best possible version of yourself. It's not his intention to shame you into making the right choices. Or for you to shame others, for that matter.

Everything in the Scriptures and the law and the prophets comes down to this: *God wants to be with us.* Every detail has been planned and arranged meticulously throughout history from the beginning for us to be together with him so that nothing can separate us again. No sin. No fake idols. No false ideas of who he is. No other person or even spiritual being.

He even came to earth as a human and "made himself nothing by taking the very nature of a servant," as Philippians 2:7 tells us, so that he could experience life as we do and then destroy every obstacle between us that kept us from connecting with him.

Priscilla Shirer simply and effectively shares it this way in her powerful book *Fervent*: "God doesn't want something *from* you. He wants something *for* you."[2] I might add this: it's not about what you're producing for God; it's what he's producing in you.

God doesn't need anything from us. Not to be good, not to change the world, not to fix people, not to make him happy. He wants us to be with him and to help others be with him. He simply wants what is our greatest good, a reunion with the Creator who formed us and knows us intimately. Because he loves just that incredibly much.

Everything in the Scriptures and the law and the prophets comes down to this: God wants to be with us.

And he doesn't just say it or plan for it and then leave us to our own devices to figure it out. He *displayed* to us what it looks like when you love radically. When you love that much, you give everything you have. You do whatever it takes. He modeled for us the ultimate example of how you live out such an incredible love.

For so long, I'd been trying to earn and prove and do the right thing in an attempt to save myself, while all along, God has always been saying,

Come, all you who are thirsty,
   come to the waters;
and you who have no money,
   come, buy and eat!

Come, buy wine and milk
>without money and without cost.
Why spend money on what is not bread,
>and your labor on what does not satisfy?
Listen, listen to me, and eat what is good,
>and you will delight in the richest of fare.
Give ear and come to me;
>listen, that you may live.
I will make an everlasting covenant with you,
>my faithful love promised to David. (Isa. 55:1–3)

And his invitation echoes in the words of Jesus, Son of God and God embodied and our salvation, again and again: Come to me …

For rest and relief: "Come to me, all you who are weary and burdened, and I will give you rest" (Matt. 11:28).

For a firm foundation and way of life: "As for everyone who comes to me and hears my words and puts them into practice, I will show you what they are like. They are like a man building a house, who dug down deep and laid the foundation on rock. When a flood came, the torrent struck that house but could not shake it, because it was well built" (Luke 6:47–48).

For eternal life: "You study the Scriptures diligently because you think that in them you have eternal life. These are the very Scriptures that testify about me, yet you refuse to come to me to have life" (John 5:39–40).

For nourishment: "I am the bread of life. Whoever comes to me will never go hungry, and whoever believes in me will never be thirsty" (John 6:35).

To be raised up, according to God's will: "All those the Father gives me will come to me, and whoever comes to me I will never drive away. For I have come down from heaven not to do my will but to do the will of him who sent me. And this is the will of him who sent me, that I shall lose none of all those he has given me, but raise them up at the last day" (John 6:37–39).

This is grace: God loves us so much he tears down any barrier that keeps us from him. Even our own senseless selves. Even our own sin. He calls us worthy and his own. He reconciles us to a relationship with him, meaning we can live out our purpose, our greatest good, and our God-given identity.

My favorite image of God in the whole Bible is the one from Jesus' parable of the lost son in Luke 15. We know the son's treatment of the father: Disowning. Disrespectful. Dismissive. The son takes his inheritance and goes to live on his own terms. Later, upon finding himself broke and broken, hungry and humbled, he makes his way home to nervously approach his father. That same father, who is waiting and watching for him, sprints frantically out to meet him—probably looking completely ridiculous because, let's be fair, that's most of us when we run—and throws his arms out for a giant embrace. They feast and celebrate that night over a lost son found.

Jesus made it a point to let us know exactly what kind of heart our Father has toward us. There can be no confusion. God loves a good comeback. And no matter how far we go, we can never run too far from him.

This is the point that changes everything. When I caught up to the magnitude of God's grace, then the whole list of things I'd done to earn my salvation (like sharing my faith, praying, and reading my Bible) became things that simply over-flowed out of me. *Look at what God did! Look at how he tears down barriers to get to us! Praise God! Grace upon grace! Nothing I could do for him would be too little.*

> *God loves a good comeback. And no matter how far we go, we can never run too far from him.*

Satan wants to mar your perspective of grace, your relationship with God, and your view of the people around you. Your Enemy would rather you find your identity in your works, accomplishments, goals, possessions—anywhere but God. He would love for you to get lost in your own head when it comes to making God known, allowing judgments, assumptions, and insecurities to win out instead. He'd like to make "sharing your faith" a task on your to-do list, more about your own self-righteousness than about love. When our eyes are on ourselves, our mission seems huge, intimidating, impossible.

This is why we take on the full armor of God, so we are able to take our stand against the Devil's schemes. Let's fight with all we have the Devil's intentions to keep us quiet and grace small, instead focusing on the powerful impact God has purposed for us as we direct people back to him.

Love Lived Out

The Bible gives so many examples of incredible women who answered the call to spread the Word with both courage and humility. Women are a huge part of God's plan to deliver his invitation to people far and wide. We'll focus on one in particular right now: the woman Jesus met at the well of Sychar, a town in Samaria. This story is twofold: how Jesus shares with her and how she goes on to share with others. If you aren't familiar with her story, take a minute to read through John 4:1–42 before we go on.

At the beginning of her conversation with Jesus, this woman showed all the signs of being on the defensive. She was alone, drawing water from the well and carrying it home in the midday heat, rather than with groups of women at a cooler time of the day, as was customary. Approached by a man she didn't know, she had quick, sharp, direct responses. In any translation of this passage, you can sense her deflection. I can almost see her roll her eyes and hear her say, "Oh *reeeally*? Well …"

Can you blame her? We go on to find out that she was distrustful of men, having been through five marriages and currently in a relationship with an undefined status. She was distrustful enough of others in her town to avoid them, even if it made life more difficult for her. She was distrustful of Jews, as were all Samaritans—a distrust built over generations of conflict and contempt. We don't have specific evidence of it, but you might guess she was distrustful of God too.

Day after day, she dutifully went to the well. Day after day, she was still thirsty.

Based on personal experience, this woman probably viewed most people as adversaries. No wonder she seemed out to protect and prove herself. She was hurting. She felt alone. She was desperate, pursuing wholeness but not finding it. She put up walls, even walls of religion. She had yet to see all that Jesus was offering her. She had yet to accept this invitation of all-encompassing grace and love God extended to her. Does any of this sound familiar at all?

"If only you knew …" Jesus told her. In other words, "If you knew the gift of God," or "the generosity of God," as *The Message* words it in verse 10. Here's what

Jesus was communicating: "If you knew who was talking with you, if you knew what he was offering, if you knew, then none of these other questions or walls or fears would even be an issue. You would find just what you're looking for. You wouldn't be thirsty anymore.

Jesus loves and longs for this work of breaking down walls, reconciling people to God, and handing out God's invitation to eternal life that starts right here and now.

Jesus wasn't put off by the woman's disdain. He saw past her fears and barriers, and he kindly and patiently offered her living water. Echoes of earlier words come to mind: *"Come, all you who are thirsty, come to the waters ..."* There was straightforward talk about her current situation, without shame or accusation. There was an explanation of the future of religion and relationship—that all will be able to come before God to worship "in the Spirit and in truth" (v. 23).

Spirit and truth, meaning, "as you are." Not adjusting your appearance or cleaning up your act or being at the right place at the right time. No matter what you've done or where you've been. All are invited. All can receive the living water freely.

This was a message that would not have been lost on this particular woman, so overwhelmed by all the barriers in her life that kept her from true freedom.

It's clear that this was soul-satisfying work for Jesus—his "food," as he later told his disciples in verse 34. Jesus loves and longs for this work of breaking down walls, reconciling people to God, and handing out God's invitation to eternal life that starts right here and now. It's the same joy we can find in extending God's invitation to others. It's not just an invitation to church.

And then Jesus made the big reveal in verses 25–26:

> The woman said, "I know that Messiah" (called Christ) "is com-
> ing. When he comes, he will explain everything to us."
> Then Jesus declared, "I, the one speaking to you—I am he."

In all the Gospels, this woman is one of the first and few people to whom Jesus openly acknowledged that he was the Christ, the Messiah. Why reveal himself to her? She was unaccepted by the town, kept to herself, and had a past. Also, she was a woman and a Samaritan.

Jesus' revelation was part of her restoration. She was no longer hiding from her town or covering up the things she used to be ashamed of. "Come, see a man who told me everything I ever did," she exclaimed (v. 29). And the whole town, astonished by this woman's testimony (and, I assume, her changed attitude) made their way out to the well to meet Jesus too.

I love the creative portrayal of this biblical moment in the series *The Chosen*, in season 1, episode 8.[3] Jesus had humor in his eyes as he engaged with the woman at the well. You can see how his heart went out to her, not wanting her to leave until she understood. And once she did, everything about her demeanor changed. I cried when I saw her joyfully leap off to spread the news across town.

Anyone can extend this invitation. Anyone can receive it. Everyone who has experienced God's transforming, redemptive grace and love has a story to share and a Messiah to show others.

It's Not Up to You—in the Best Way

What if, halfway down the hill on her way to tell the town, the Samaritan woman started having second thoughts?

> *Did that really happen? Is he really the Messiah?*
> *What if people laugh at me? What if I can't convince them?*
> *Who would believe me anyway? I'm nobody.*

By the time she made it down the hill, she might have nervously looked around her and slipped back home before anyone was the wiser. The story would have ended a lot differently. Maybe we never would have heard it.

Why didn't she change her mind? Because Jesus changed everything. It was no longer about her shortcomings or fears. There was no turning back. Just that one conversation left her convinced, her questions answered, her hope fulfilled.

Why do we change our minds when it comes to spreading the good news? We start asking questions: *Who am I to talk about this? What if I make a fool of myself? Who would listen to me? What do I have to offer?* Slowly we reconsider and become quiet.

Satan would love to silence you. Both because it leaves you inoperative—and because those fears are blatant lies. The kind of lies he loves to tell.

The truth is, sharing our faith and making God known isn't about us at all. It's not about what we have to offer (or what we feel we don't). And it's not our job to grow anything in anyone else's heart.

Growing up, I was convinced it all fell on me. The only way to save someone was to have the best questions that cut to the heart, the strongest arguments to defend the Scriptures, and the wisest words to prompt action. Finding myself often falling short of that, I would shrink back, silent. Or, in trying to muster up my own confidence, I would lack the kind of love that God demonstrates to us.

One of my heroes in the faith, Paul, had the clearest vision of his role in all of this. Although we credit him with planting and strengthening many early churches, spreading the gospel, and writing some of the most memorable Scriptures, he freely admits where he falls short: "My message and my preaching were not with wise and persuasive words, but with a demonstration of the Spirit's power, so that your faith might not rest on human wisdom, but on God's power" (1 Cor. 2:4–5).

There was nothing Paul had that we don't (except that incredible encounter with Jesus himself). It's all the grace of Jesus. "In him you have been enriched in every way—with all kinds of speech and with all knowledge—God thus confirming our testimony about Christ among you. Therefore you do not lack any spiritual gift as you eagerly wait for our Lord Jesus Christ to be revealed" (1:5–7).

Did you catch that? We are enriched in every way. Our testimony about Christ is confirmed by God. We don't lack any spiritual gifts.

- Through the Scriptures, we are equipped to do God's work (2 Tim. 3:16–17).
- We have the Spirit of God and the mind of Christ (1 Cor. 2:13–16).
- We are created to do the good works God prepared for us (Eph. 2:10).
- Through God's power, we have everything we need to live godly lives (2 Pet. 1:3).

- The Spirit distributes gifts to us, and we work together to use them for the body of Christ (1 Cor. 12:7, 12).

And as we see with the Samaritan woman and so many others in Scripture, just an experience of being with Christ is a testimony that can make an impact.

You are so much more equipped and supported than you realize. And yet, it's still not up to you. You don't have to be Paul to be used by God because, again, it's not about you. It's about what God is working through you.

Paul knew this and didn't give himself the credit.

> Neither the one who plants nor the one who waters is anything, but only God, who makes things grow. The one who plants and the one who waters have one purpose, and they will each be rewarded according to their own labor. For we are co-workers in God's service; you are God's field, God's building. (1 Cor. 3:7–9)

This goes back to Jesus' original instruction to his disciples in John 15: "I am the vine; you are the branches. If you remain in me and I in you, you will bear much fruit; apart from me you can do nothing.… This is to my Father's glory, that you bear much fruit, showing yourselves to be my disciples" (vv. 5, 8).

The pressure off of us is twofold—it is not about our elaborate explanations or wisdom, and it's not about our own power at work. God does the work. We remain in him, and we show up with willing hearts.

Even more, there is a release of control about how people respond to us, for better or for worse. It's not a face-off against a potential enemy or another number to add to the flock. Our role is to simply be faithful to what God asks us to do. He takes care of the rest.

Go back to the Samaritan woman. Can you imagine her joy as she went to tell the rest of her town this incredible thing? That the Son of God who would save the world came to speak to her? That her past and reputation didn't matter to him? That he welcomed and invited her to the love and grace and living water that God invites us all to experience?

All of this same joy is held out to you. The same love and grace. Drink it up, friend. And then pass it on.

Let's Do This

Write down the story of your own encounter(s) with Jesus, like the Samaritan woman. Note when you realized Jesus was the answer for what you had been seeking and what it was about your experience that transformed you. Consider your before and after picture with Jesus.

Work It Out

1. What does God's invitation mean to you? How has it changed your life?

_____

_____

_____

_____

_____

_____

_____

_____

_____

_____

_____

_____

_____

_____

_____

_____

_____

_____

_____

_____

_____

_____

_____

_____

2. List some ways nonbelievers can feel like the enemy. Have your experiences left you hesitant to share your faith? Find a trustworthy ally with whom you can share these experiences, and together find healthy ways to break down barriers that may have formed.

3. From the Scriptures, what are ways we are equipped and empowered by God to spread his message and invitation to others? In your own experience, what are some of the gifts he's given you to be able to build his kingdom?

Three truths I know about God

- ◆
- ◆
- ◆

Three things I'm grateful for

- ◆
- ◆
- ◆

Three steps I can take moving forward

- ◆
- ◆
- ◆

Watch Video 5

Find the link on page 28.

Video Notes

Reflective Prayer

Prayer Requests

Praises

Chapter 6

The Woman Who Has It All Together

More than 298,000 followers gawked at twenty-six-year-old Natalia Taylor's glamorous snapshots set in a vintage, expensive-looking hotel.

Wearing thick gold hoops and a hot-pink dress, this influencer with hundreds of thousands of followers took on several graceful poses: Ordering room service on a turquoise phone. Glancing over her shoulder from a vanity. Popping champagne in a sleek kitchen. Adjusting her stiletto while sitting on a wooden lawn chair.

All the photos were tagged Bali, Indonesia. It looked like the perfect vacation—one of those extravagant ones that wouldn't be out of place among the A-list crowd. Except … she wasn't in Bali. Not even close.

Days later on her YouTube channel, Natalia surprised her followers with the following revelation: it was all a prank. She actually set up the whole photo shoot with a photographer friend *in the showrooms of the budget-friendly home superstore IKEA*. (#unsponsored)

Natalia also revealed that she timed the posting of the photos with strategic Instagram stories (videos and snapshots that publicly disappear after twenty-four hours) of travel videos taken from the internet, borrowed from friends, or filmed covertly at IKEA. It was all an attempt to make followers fall for the story that she had recently landed in Indonesia for a luxurious holiday.

She's one of the honest ones. With photography tricks, editing applications, and a little social media savvy, people can (and sometimes do) fabricate whatever image they want to deliver. "Life on the internet isn't always what it seems, especially in this day and age where it's so easy to pretend to be anyone you want to be," says Natalia in her video.[1]

Or, as the viral jingle by Ben Rector goes, "I don't know who needs to hear this, but the internet isn't real life."[2]

We know it. Even as we scroll, we realize the internet affects the way we think about ourselves and others. Studies show that it alters our perspective of what is actually real and valuable and attainable and can wound our self-esteem and mental health. News stories and streaming shows expose influencer scams for money, publicity, followers, and likes. We know all this.

And yet.

What if we stopped worshipping the idol of perfection as a measurement of our own validation in our lives? What if we stopped falling for the lie of perfection in someone else's?

Yet we spend hours scrolling through our feeds. We gaze at flawless photos and videos. We fill up on photos of perfect houses, products we can't afford, impossibly gorgeous and peaceful family photos, and exciting life or career news; then we unsurprisingly leave social media feeling distracted, lonely, and self-critical. And then we dive back in for more. Sometimes even we may be guilty of sharing the highlights and shading the reality.

Social media itself isn't the enemy. Neither is the woman with the flawless white-marble kitchen, the cute and attentive husband, the enviably well-behaved and talented children, the glamorous job or vacation, the fanciest purse and shoes, the funniest or most poignant words, the cutest pet, the coolest background story, or whatever image is plastered online. But the Enemy can absolutely use social media. And he does.

As a self-curated public presentation that can virtually erase pesky weaknesses, social media is one of many ways we try to provide the answers we are so desperately seeking: *Do you see all that I'm doing? Do you see how hard I'm trying? Do you see me? Am I lovable? Am I acceptable? Am I enough?*

Even if we're not looking for the answers in social media, there's a number of other places we can attempt to find them: magazines, movies, careers, awards, reviews, numbers, money, possessions. A hunger gnaws away to fill that insecurity anywhere we can.

Our society is addicted to the image of having it all together. And yet those standards are based on a level of perfection that isn't real. If our lives aren't "perfect" like someone else's appears to be, we become skeptical of God and his goodness, of who he's made us to be.

What if we stopped worshipping the idol of perfection as a measurement of our own validation in our lives? What if we stopped falling for the lie of perfection in someone else's?

Friend, for every question you have about your identity, God has already answered each one for you. Every single one that establishes your worth and affirmation. When those questions are answered, we don't have to prove them for ourselves or find them in relation to an image of how someone else is (supposedly) doing. We certainly don't have to stage a fake identity or photo shoot. In spite of our lack, we actually have it all. Though not necessarily all together.

Something to Prove?

There may not be another group of people in the Bible so laughably relatable as Jesus' disciples.

They argued about who was greater. They scratched their heads over his teachings. After witnessing firsthand the incredible miracles Jesus performed, they still panicked when confronted with challenges. In short, they were just like us—and thankfully so. Their humanity is not only relatable but makes the clarity and grace in Jesus' words and actions shine all the more.

One apostle is mentioned in the Gospels more times than all the others. Long before he held the keys to the kingdom, he started in the very best place any of us can begin: humbled by his lack of perfection, his hands open, with nothing to offer.

It started with a miraculous catch of fish after a full night of empty nets. Stunned, the fisherman Simon fell on his knees before Jesus. "Go away from me, Lord; I am a sinful man!" (Luke 5:8). Instead of shrugging his shoulders in agreement and keeping his distance, Jesus calmed the fisherman's fears and told him to follow along and learn to catch people instead. Without a second thought, Simon and his companions left everything else behind to go.

The most important and crucial detail about Simon (whom Jesus later began calling Peter) is that he knew how much he needed God. It's what motivated him to literally drop everything and follow Jesus, prompting a complete transformation in his life. He became arguably one of Jesus' closest friends and one of the most notable early church leaders, and I wonder if that was partially because he understood how much he needed Jesus.

Peter's faith helped him realize heavenly things that so many of the people around him missed; it allowed him to take incredible steps of boldness and eventually start the church in the days after Jesus. He's one of our forefathers in faith. But he's also incredibly relatable, and you might notice that in some of these accounts, it seems he has something to prove.

- He was the only one of the disciples to ask Jesus if he could walk on water (see Matt. 14:25–31).
- He offered to build a structure for Jesus, Elijah, and Moses at the transfiguration (see Matt. 17:1–5).
- He brought a sword and sliced off a servant's ear as soldiers approached to arrest Jesus. (See John 18:10–11. I find it a little amusing that the other accounts avoid naming Simon Peter, but John calls him out. You'll notice a bit of a rivalry between Simon Peter and John.)
- He boasted that he would never leave Jesus, to the point of dying, but later hid in a courtyard and denied association with Jesus when others confronted him (see Matt. 26:31–35, 69–74).
- He raced another disciple while attempting to be the first to enter Jesus' tomb. (See John 20:3–7. Notice that rivalry with John again?)
- He leaped out of the boat to run to the newly raised Jesus on the shore while the other disciples rowed back (see John 21:7).
- He had to overcome prejudices (with God's help) to visit the home of Cornelius (see Acts 10:9–35).

- He felt the scrutiny of the Jews in the presence of the Gentiles and acted differently when they were around (see Gal. 2:11–13).

In one significant story, Peter makes a huge declaration of faith and then goes on to rebuke and be rebuked by Jesus, all within several verses of each other in Matthew 16:15–23:

"But what about you?" he asked. "Who do you say I am?"

Simon Peter answered, "You are the Messiah, the Son of the living God."

Jesus replied, "Blessed are you, Simon son of Jonah, for this was not revealed to you by flesh and blood, but by my Father in heaven. And I tell you that you are Peter, and on this rock I will build my church, and the gates of Hades will not overcome it. I will give you the keys of the kingdom of heaven; whatever you bind on earth will be bound in heaven, and whatever you loose on earth will be loosed in heaven." Then he ordered his disciples not to tell anyone that he was the Messiah.

From that time on Jesus began to explain to his disciples that he must go to Jerusalem and suffer many things at the hands of the elders, the chief priests and the teachers of the law, and that he must be killed and on the third day be raised to life.

Peter took him aside and began to rebuke him. "Never, Lord!" he said. "This shall never happen to you!"

Jesus turned and said to Peter, "Get behind me, Satan! You are a stumbling block to me; you do not have in mind the concerns of God, but merely human concerns."

Did you get whiplash from how quickly that situation turned on Peter? From making one of the earliest declarations of Jesus as Messiah and being handed the keys to the kingdom to being called Satan.

Many commentators point out the fact that while Peter grasped something important—that Jesus is the Christ—he missed entirely what that meant. He assumed, as did many, that Jesus was coming to break the Jews free from Roman oppression and become the new king of the Jews … whereas Jesus always knew what he really came to do—to become the King of Kings, much higher and more powerful than any earthly one, and to defeat sin and Satan once and for all, releasing us from a fear of death and giving us eternal open access to a God who loves us. The weight of that mission was heavy, and Jesus needed no prompting to deviate from it. No wonder sparks flew.

Notice Jesus' words: "You do not have in mind the concerns of God, but merely human concerns" (v. 23). Satan was happy to distract Jesus with earthly matters if it meant he could win over him (and us) for eternity. Jesus would have none of it, as he was well aware of the deceit and strategy of the Enemy.

Here's what we know about some of the Devil's tactics when he attacked the Son of God at various points in Scripture: Satan got him alone. He manipulated the Word for his own benefit. And here's the kicker: he tried to get Jesus to *prove* his status as the Son of God (that is to say, equal to God) by displaying his power. (All this can be found in Matt. 4:1–11.)

From the very start, in the garden of Eden, Satan has been trying to play the same game with humans. Based on what he told Eve, each of us could be "like God" (Gen. 3:5), *even though God already designed us in his image.* Satan wants us to deny our true identity and force us into the bondage of proving something that *is already established.* He'd prefer our attention divided, our insecurities flared, and other people's opinions and approval to be more important.

Jesus didn't fall for that. If the Enemy could even manipulate Scripture in the battle of the cross for the salvation of our souls, then he could easily do the same to Jesus' contemporaries, followers, and even his closest friends: "Jesus would not entrust himself to them, for he knew all people. He did not need any testimony about mankind, for he knew what was in each person" (John 2:24–25).

You and I have every reason to be as confident as Jesus in who we are and whose we are. Our identities, worth, and purpose have been established by God, our righteousness established by Jesus through his death, burial, and resurrection. (If you need more of this confidence, we'll get there in chapter 9.)

Thank God Jesus didn't fall for Satan's lies (even as they came through his friend Simon Peter). His choice to stick to God's perfect plan means redemption, salvation, and confidence for us all.

Let's make note of one more thing about Simon. Before he declared Jesus as the Christ, before he walked on water or raised the dead or preached a sermon that resulted in three thousand people getting baptized, Jesus handed him a new name.

> Andrew, Simon Peter's brother, was one of the two who heard what John had said and who had followed Jesus. The first thing Andrew did was to find his brother Simon and tell him, "We have found the Messiah" (that is, the Christ). And he brought him to Jesus.
>
> Jesus looked at him and said, "You are Simon son of John. You will be called Cephas" (which, when translated, is Peter). (John 1:40–42)

The name Simon in Hebrew can mean "to hear, be heard" and "reputation,"[3] or "a hearing."[4] Both Cephas and Peter mean "rock." As we read above, Jesus declared that Peter would now be the rock upon which the church was built. Even the gates of Hades would not overcome it. Surely no one on this earth could steal that identity either.

Jesus literally changed Simon's identity by changing his name—from needing to be concerned with reputation or being heard to being a solid rock and the foundation of the church.

Trash to Treasure

If you're seeking out another example of a dramatic turnaround, look no further than the apostle Paul, formerly known as Saul. (Another significant name change that came after an encounter with Jesus!)

Paul had it all together, spiritually speaking, in the time of the Pharisees and Romans:

> If someone else thinks they have reasons to put confidence in the flesh, I have more: circumcised on the eighth day, of the people of Israel, of the tribe of Benjamin, a Hebrew of Hebrews; in regard to the law, a Pharisee; as for zeal, persecuting the church; as for righteousness based on the law, faultless. (Phil. 3:4–6)

If he was applying for the role of Best Hebrew, Paul would have gotten the job. His resume showed that everything was in order: circumcised as a newborn in the proper time according to God's covenant with his people, a traceable Jewish ancestry, authority as a teacher who was imprisoning and killing people in God's name, and a record of keeping the commandments faultlessly—at least according to the law. (I appreciate that he specifies that point!)

These qualifications he so easily rattles off appear to be things he formerly took great pride in, a collection of accomplishments he must have polished regularly in his pre-Jesus days. He perhaps wielded them as weapons, ready to both intimidate others while defending his own good standing before God and people.

These are only conjectures about Paul. I guess at this because I relate to a protective line of thinking—namely, the easy answers I often would fall back on to maintain my status as a "good girl" while holding people at a distance. *I grew up going to church. I was baptized at age twelve. I get good grades. I don't get into trouble.* Later it became the more acceptable adult version: *It's fine. I'm fine. I've got this. I'm working on it. Here's what I read in my Bible today. Here are some good things I'm doing.* These would excuse my internal battles with insecurity and even my judgments and self-righteousness toward other people.

And then Paul turns every defense he used to have on its head (here in Eugene Peterson's paraphrase):

> The very credentials these people are waving around as something special, I'm tearing up and throwing out with the trash—along with everything else I used to take credit for. And why? Because of Christ. Yes, all the things I once thought were so important are gone from my life. Compared to the high privilege of knowing Christ Jesus as my Master, firsthand, everything I once thought I had going for me is insignificant—dog dung. I've dumped it all in the trash so that I could embrace Christ and be embraced by him. I didn't want some petty, inferior brand of righteousness that comes from keeping a list of rules when I could get the robust kind that comes from trusting Christ—*God's* righteousness. (Phil. 3:7–9 MSG)

With this declaration, Paul sets us free from the demands of meeting a worldly checklist, running the hamster wheel of striving, and competing with others who are either succeeding or failing in our eyes. And if we let it, this perspective can set others free from the judgments and limitations we place on them too.

Because *it's all garbage*: the claims we make, the yardsticks we use to measure worth, the resumes, the pedestals, everything that would recommend us here in this society with glowing reviews. Even the pretty walls we build to keep people out. Trash. It's all loss compared to the restorative righteousness and overwhelming grace and unbelievably full life that God provides through Jesus.

One of my kids used to be obsessed with all things garbage. His eyes would light up as he heard trash trucks roll down the street, and he would go running to the window, pressing his little nose against the glass, to see them in all their glory. We read numerous books on trash trucks. I bought him a pencil cup at the dollar store that was shaped like a garbage bin, which he played with like a toy. And after trying to inspect various trash cans and being told to keep his distance, he came up with his own little chant: "Trashy! No touchy! Trashy! No touchy!" Even something he couldn't have felt magical to him.

Not unlike my former toddler, we've stumbled upon trash and called it treasure. We're fascinated by things that shine, but those are things that also happen to mold, decay, diminish in value, break, or get stolen. We take items out of the garbage can ("Trashy! No touchy!") and dress ourselves in them, becoming identified by the debris.

We are highly prizing the wrong things. No wonder we feel needless competition with others who either have what we want or don't. And it's no surprise that we don't feel satisfied when we achieve what we thought we wanted on this earth.

Again, Paul said he was faultless when it came to the law. But then here in verses 8–9, he says he is giving up his old ways of striving and fully embracing a righteousness that comes freely from God. His greatest treasures are knowing Jesus, gaining Jesus, and being found in Jesus.

Prove It

To prove something is to test and display the validity of a claim. You only have to prove something when the details are in question. But who gets to decide that your identity is up for debate? You? The people around you? The Enemy?

When our worth feels in question and there is something we have to prove, we hold people at arm's length to keep them from seeing the things that make us ashamed. We split our personalities and wear masks, only showing what we want people to see, and become paranoid that our real selves will be revealed.

When there is something we have to prove, we substitute fake intimacy for real. We feel shame, inadequacy, and inferiority, so we hold people at a distance. We even start to see them as the enemy, people who threaten to unmask us and expose those shortcomings we are so desperate to hide.

> Validation doesn't come from making yourself believe in how great you are. It comes from being deeply rooted in who God says you are.

When we feel there is something we have to prove, we're settling for less than the fullness God is offering, less than the complete picture, less than whole communication and relationships. We assume that the other woman has bad intentions to expose and humiliate us. She becomes suspicious and sneaky and unreliable. In this divide, Satan can and will manipulate that to isolate and destroy us.

All the while, God is patiently waiting, arms open wide to catch us for the day ours give out. He has written an invitation unlike any other: *Come, give up your striving and proving. Trust in my faithfulness and goodness. Wholeheartedly accept the identity I have already established for you.*

Should we love the person God made us to be and take responsibility for ourselves? *Yes.* Can we prove and self-love our way through feelings of inadequacy? *No.*

We are wired for approval—we just tend to seek it from the wrong places. Validation doesn't come from making yourself believe in how great you are. It comes from being deeply rooted in who God says you are. He is completely trustworthy. You are completely loved.

When it comes to the settling of our identity, let's instead hand over that responsibility to the Designer and Creator of the earth and everything in it. Read the following passage, and then read it again until the fact sinks in: these words are about you specifically.

> Long before he laid down earth's foundations, he had us in mind, had settled on us as the focus of his love, to be made whole and holy by his love. Long, long ago he decided to adopt us into his family through Jesus Christ. (What pleasure he took in planning this!) He wanted us to enter into the celebration of his lavish gift-giving by the hand of his beloved Son.
>
> Because of the sacrifice of the Messiah, his blood poured out on the altar of the Cross, we're a free people—free of penalties and punishments chalked up by all our misdeeds. And not just barely free, either. *Abundantly* free! He thought of everything, provided for everything we could possibly need, letting us in on the plans he took such delight in making. He set it all out before us in Christ, a long-range plan in which everything would be brought together

and summed up in him, everything in deepest heaven, everything
on planet earth. (Eph. 1:4–10 MSG)

Everything you're wondering about yourself, you already are. You are already
seen, loved, accepted, approved, equipped, and empowered.

You are already pleasing to God. Sinning less or doing more—neither one
makes us become pleasing to God.

You are already chosen and purposed to use the skills and talents God gave you
to do his work in this world. You are already approved for this work—no need to
obtain approval.

When we decide God is who he says he is and we are who he says we are, we
are freed to be ourselves in real life *and* online. This truth releases us from the toxic
need to compete with a perfect image that doesn't exist.

And when it comes to other people, this truth becomes a way of seeing past
those smoke screens of "perfect lives" and the masks of "perfect faces." We can
become safe places and open arms to women who have only ever known a need to
hide and prove. Let's look into this a little bit more in the next chapter.

Let's Do This

Assess your time on social media (or wherever you most often turn for validation). Determine a length of time you could release it for a sabbatical—maybe a day, week, or month—and observe what happens when you do. Consider making it a regular event. Take this time to journal and reflect on how it is affecting you.

Work It Out

1. What does the woman look like who has it all together, in your opinion? What makes her life seem perfect? Why does that feel threatening to you? What does God's Word say about who you are? What does God say about who she is?

_____

_____

_____

_____

_____

_____

_____

_____

_____

_____

_____

_____

_____

_____

_____

_____

_____

2. What are your typical habits when you feel the need to prove yourself? What does God's Word say about who you are? What does it say about who she is?

3. Write out God's personal invitation for you when it comes to his and your identities. What questions is he inviting you to put to rest in him?

Three truths I know about God

Three things I'm grateful for

Three steps I can take moving forward

Find the link on page 28.

Video Notes

_____

_____

_____

_____

_____

_____

_____

_____

_____

_____

_____

_____

_____

_____

_____

_____

_____

_____

_____

_____

Reflective Prayer

Prayer Requests

Praises

Chapter 7

The Woman Who Has Guardrails Up

Society glorifies people who "have it all together," a concept we talked about in the last chapter. But, if we're honest, there's something magical and alluring about this persona; being independent in this way seems like a pretty secure place to be. If you have it all together, you don't have to let anyone else in. No one needs to question, doubt, worry about, or help someone who has their act together or has it all figured out.

It's sensitive and risky to need people. It hurts when they let you down. Society tells us not to be too "needy," making getting help from others out to be weakness instead of strength. People project one unapproachable image to the world, then quietly suffer in reality behind closed doors. And Satan cheers all of this on.

Being unreachable or inaccessible can come in all kinds of forms: grumpy and dismissive, angry, self-obsessed, quiet and introverted, goofy or foolish, too busy for anything, unattainably smart or witty, exceedingly helpful and generous, or rebellious. And lest we think we're safe from more worldly characteristics: religious practices and lifestyles can be things we hide behind too.

On their own, these characteristics are simply part of what makes up our personalities. It's when they're in place to distract and deflect that they become walls of self-defense, doing their best to keep people out. This seems to be a sensible way to avoid pain and heartbreak, but it rarely works. Independence and self-sufficiency are deeply lonely and powerful deceptions.

The woman who keeps everyone out can feel like the enemy. You know who I mean—the one who intimidatingly takes charge of all the things at work or church maybe, or the one who keeps to herself and doesn't appear to care what anyone thinks. She could be the one who is always immaculately dressed or laughs so readily at her own faults that shame seems nonexistent for her. The one who appears too proud or independent or stoic, her personality too big to need someone like you. Someone stuck in her own ways, whose mind can't be changed, who can't and won't be helped. Interactions with her leave us feeling edged out, belittled, and useless. Why bother pursuing the relationship further?

Those who appear invulnerable may feel like they have something to prove, just as we talked about in the last chapter—seeking validation. But they also may have something to protect—their reputations, relationships, goals, history, shortcomings, even their authentic selves. It's a product of scarcity or shame-based thinking. *If they knew this about me, they would judge me. If they saw me as I really am, they would hate me. No one else deals with this. I can handle it on my own. I don't want to burden anyone else with my problems. It's best to keep it hidden.*

How tragically ironic that almost all of us experience thoughts like these and yet truly believe we're completely on our own.

Satan's fingerprints are all over this strategy, making you believe that those with guardrails up are lost causes, either not needing or not worthy of your love, concern, time, or energy. He wants you to write her off.

What's the remedy for self-protection? It's vulnerability. Choosing vulnerability means sharing the weaknesses, fears, and doubts in our own lives and cultivating secure spaces for others to be able to do the same. Author and speaker Ann Voskamp had these powerful words to share on her Facebook page: "Shame gets unspeakable power only if it's unspeakable. *Shame dies when stories are told in safe places.*"[1]

No matter what someone projects to the world, there is always another side to the story that you don't know. It might be the bristly boss who actually comes through with a kind heart, the arrogant prima donna with the painful family life, or the eccentric influencer who is so much more resilient and generous than the world expects her to be.

When we keep pursuing people and granting them permission to show up authentically (not unlike God does for us), they have the opportunity to be completely themselves. They have the chance to surprise us with vulnerability, generosity, and hope. That's what we're going to talk about in this chapter: how to be a friend who leans in instead of avoiding the woman with the guardrails up.

Least Questions Asked

My self-protection is award-winning. I'm not kidding.

In college I took a sewing class, which concluded with a self-designed outfit we had to model in an end-of-semester fashion show, along with an awards ceremony complete with homemade sashes. My award? "Least Questions Asked." As in, I kept to myself and barely spoke a word all semester. Yes, I would have rather redone a whole hemline than ask for help from the *professors* who were there to *teach us*. Thank you, thank you very much.

I was simply following the plan I'd laid out for my life—to be the one who tried never to draw attention to herself, need help, or look foolish or weak. Maybe if I could keep from letting others in and be smart and capable enough on my own, no one would ever tell how much I was failing.

It happened with ballet, quitting despite my love for it because I was more round and less graceful than most of the other ballerinas; with math classes, when I settled for a lower grade rather than show up for extra help; when I begged my mom not to tell anyone I was seeing a psychiatrist for my depression, afraid people would find out how broken I was; and when I lost my job as a nanny because I didn't want to appear incompetent by asking for more information.

As you might imagine, the same attitude applied to my faith journey from a young age. The Bible more often meant a list of rules from a demanding God, and I was constantly falling short of one and letting down the other. Grace played a small role. Shame was the much bigger motivation.

My walls were always up around other people because, again, if I was failing, I didn't want anyone to know. I was terrified of being labeled as weak and never wanted to give anyone the chance to question my goodness, dedication, or faith. Instead, armed with correct answers and behavior, I became the goody-goody no one ever needed to worry about—and, unsurprisingly, the one most of my peers avoided (not that I blame them). I'm sure I passed my anxiety, paranoia, and exhaustion on to others, and I regret it. Unsurprisingly, my arms grew weary from trying to hold it all together, and it broke me.

I tried to look like I had it all together, but it wasn't at all true. If I'd been left to my own devices in that space of stubborn self-defense, I would still be stuck in that place. Instead, God provided people who were willing to show up for me in the mess, allow me to be truly honest and genuine about where I was, and help point me back to him. God's nature and desire are not to leave us stuck in our brokenness and our fears but to bring us close to one another, even in the midst of these.

Let's look at some examples and ideas for letting our own guardrails down and allowing others to show up authentically.

Allow Room for Questions and Doubts

Society tends to value being certain and absolute while associating nuance and questions with being wishy-washy or weak. (Funny, for a society that also promotes achieving balance.)

When it comes to faith, it's the opposite. God invites us to wonder, wander, and wrestle. Faith means an ebbing, flowing, ever-growing relationship, not the measuring tape of how well we're doing or how hard we're trying with God. *If I were more faithful, this wouldn't be a struggle. If I were more faithful, I wouldn't have doubts. If I were more faithful, everything would be fine.* Shame and striving are the result of this thinking (and sometimes also the cause).

God releases us from the pressure of certainty. He understands our humanity and doubts, and we can do the same for one another.

Luke 7 provides an example of wrestling with doubts that is so moving to me. John the Baptist sends messengers to Jesus asking in verse 19, "Are you the one who is to come, or should we expect someone else?"

You know, John the Baptist. Super-zealous trailblazer for the Messiah, calling for repentance and going head-to-head with Pharisees and tax collectors. Baptizer of Jesus and witness of God's audible announcement that this was his Son. Jesus' actual cousin. If anyone should be certain, it's probably him.

Jesus' response is so full of gentleness and grace. There is no harshness here, nor a direct answer. Here's what he says in Luke 7:22–23: "Go back and report to John what you have seen and heard: The blind receive sight, the lame walk, those who have leprosy are cleansed, the deaf hear, the dead are raised, and the good news is proclaimed to the poor. Blessed is anyone who does not stumble on account of me."

God invites us to wonder, wander, and wrestle. Faith means an ebbing, flowing, ever-growing relationship.

When I was in high school, I experienced a season of reassessing my faith. Our church was confronted with serious issues and changes at that point, and it led me to questions. Who was I living my life for? Were my beliefs based on what other people told me, or on the Scriptures? Was our church community safe and biblically sound?

Fortunately in this season, I had Cara, a teen leader and mentor who took the time to hear me out about my concerns and wasn't afraid of my questions. I was also going through depression, and she became a safe person to talk to, helping me work through it when sharing with most people felt daunting.

Condemnation doesn't go together with questions and wonder. Condemnation isn't even in Christ's vocabulary. (See Rom. 8:1.) To be a safe place for someone, let's be open to their questions and concerns and always point them back to the truth. (More to come on that.)

Encourage One Another Daily

Have you ever said a word so much that it ends up sounding odd and losing its meaning for you? That experience is called semantic satiation, and sometimes it happens to me with certain buzzwords heard at church or read a number of times in Scripture.

Encouragement is one of them. It's not just a nice card or gift or a thoughtful text message. *Encouragement* means "giving someone support, confidence, or hope" and can also mean "persuasion to do or to continue something," as noted in the *Oxford English Dictionary.*[2] In my experience, encouragement is a bolster of strength in times of weakness, a heartwarming display of selflessness and connection with kind friends, or a nudge in the right direction when feeling lost or disappointed.

In Hebrews, the author speaks of encouragement as a necessity in living out Christian community, not an option. Hebrews 3:13 says, "Encourage one another daily, as long as it is called 'Today,' so that none of you may be hardened by sin's deceitfulness."

Similarly, we read in chapter 10:

> Let us consider how we may spur one another on toward love and good deeds, not giving up meeting together, as some are in the habit of doing, but encouraging one another—and all the more as you see the Day approaching. (vv. 24–25)

In college, depression and anxiety had moments of threatening to take me out spiritually. *No, depression and anxiety themselves are **not** sins.* But along with my depression and anxiety, I tended to isolate, hide, and neglect things that were spiritually, physically, emotionally, and mentally healthy for me. That's how "sin's deceitfulness" had an opportunity to worm its way.

My roommates at the time (Cat and Gaby) showed compassion and also didn't let me get hardened. Free-spirited Cat would, in her own loving way, poke and prod me until I got out of the apartment and interacted with the world again, even if only for a walk outside. She knew I wouldn't find joy or hope curled up under my covers all day. Likewise, Gaby sympathized with what I was feeling but didn't let me feel sorry for myself. I remember going on drives with her to yell or cry along with some tried-and-true anthems. (Not to age us, but Kelly Clarkson's *Breakaway* album was a favorite. Highly recommended for your most angsty moments.) Then we'd pray and arrive home a little more refreshed.

Encouragement prompts forward motion. Coupled with compassion, it's a way of saying, "I see and hear what you're going through; I'm also going to lend you some hope for what can be." It helps keep us in the fight when life feels overwhelming, and it's one of the reasons God designed us with community in mind.

Meet Them with Grace and Understanding

So many times, because of my own shame-centered mindset, I would assume I'd be confronted with criticism and condemnation if I were to expose my real heart to people. Sometimes it happened, and so I hid. But again and again, I was proved wrong and surprised by the grace and understanding held out to me.

Two women I admired so much were able to help me in my season of infertility, right around the same time I was navigating early marriage and trying to figure out what career path to pursue. (Basically, life felt emotional and up in the air.) Maral and Lindsay let me show up authentically, making time and space for conversation and allowing me to sob into my coffee and share my heart as needed. They also shared with me their own stories of their most vulnerable moments.

These women were a couple stages ahead of me in life, having been married longer and both already with children of their own. I so admired their lives and their faith, to the point of worrying that they would be too startled by my confessions or impatient with what felt like my broken record of fears and sorrows. But not once. They showed me practically what it was like to meet people with grace instead of judgment. I can only hope to create a similar safe space for those around me.

Meeting people with grace is no less than what Jesus does for us. Hebrews 4:15–16 notably says, "We do not have a high priest who is unable to empathize with our weaknesses, but we have one who has been tempted in every way, just as we are—yet he did not sin. Let us then approach God's throne of grace with confidence, so that we may receive mercy and find grace to help us in our time of need."

Even Jesus experienced weakness and temptation. These allowed him to make himself available to us in every way, meeting us with grace and mercy so we can be confident before God. How much more, as imperfect human beings, should we be available for each other with vulnerability, sincerity, and patience? All the more when it comes to those in life stages that vary from our own.

Point Them Back to Scripture

Every single answer we need—every promise, every direction, every bit of wisdom and insight—is found in Scripture. Not all the answers we want on this side of heaven. But all the answers we need.

And yet Scripture is not always easy to grasp, nor does it always come naturally to us to seek it out. Another way in which we need community in our lives is for others who can continually point us back to what God says.

When my anxiety and depression threatened to overwhelm me, I started sessions with a biblical counselor. They were nothing less than transformational. Those times brought clarity about my real issues—how I'd had a warped perspective of God that made him out to be a demanding boss rather than a loving Father and how I'd been running myself ragged trying to earn his favor, along with everyone else's.

After years of faulty thinking, these sessions helped me learn how to experience God's limitless love, compassion, and acceptance, along with how to return to that perspective when I started going back to my old ways of thinking. Truly a "renewing of [the] mind," as in Romans 12:2. The way this happened? Reading Scriptures and believing what they said. "Is that what the Bible actually says? Is that what Jesus lived out?" were questions my counselor constantly asked when my anxiety, perfectionism, and insecurity came out.

Psalm 19:7–8 assures us, "The law of the LORD is perfect, refreshing the soul. The statutes of the LORD are trustworthy, making wise the simple. The precepts of the LORD are right, giving joy to the heart. The commands of the LORD are radiant, giving light to the eyes." The best thing we can do for someone is point them back to the truth of the Scriptures, reminding them of who God is and what he says about them.

Forgive and Be Forgiven

Lastly, when we mess up—which we all will!—we have an opportunity to live out forgiveness, both offering and accepting it. Reconciliation is a radical thing. It's another particularly vulnerable place to be—acknowledging wrong, whether our own or someone else's, and trying to make it right.

Something as complex as forgiveness can only become comprehensible thanks to the God who offered it first. That gift happens to depend on our willingness to forgive others, which is a more-than-reasonable command from a God who doesn't hold our many sins against us. Jesus says in Matthew 6:14–15, "If you forgive other people when they sin against you, your heavenly Father will also forgive you. But if you do not forgive others their sins, your Father will not forgive your sins."

I've had plenty of experiences with forgiveness in my life, and undoubtedly many more will come. But the person I have to forgive and ask forgiveness from the most would be my husband. From silly things like petty arguments to moments of ridiculous stubbornness to targeted emotional pain. Once, early in marriage in the middle of a fight, I even walked out the door, leaving him honestly wondering if I was coming back. And even so, he has shown me God's love so clearly with his ready forgiveness, as well as loving me even in my messiest, angriest, most insecure moments. And I've had to forgive him, no matter how justified I felt at the time.

These are just a few examples. There isn't room to write all the ways people have showed up for me.

The Right Armor

What's important to us, we feel the need to defend. And every day is a battle. What does suiting up for battle look like for people?

Maybe a typical set of armor looks like this:

> A people-pleasing mask to cover emotions and true self
> A thick helmet of self-righteousness to protect opinions and
>   ideology

A chestplate of an apathetic appearance to cover the heart against
    hurt and pain
A sword of words to wield before someone else cuts first
An extra layer of impervious chain mail so that nothing can break
    through a hardened exterior defense
A dagger of sarcasm or wit to quickly deflect embarrassment or
    vulnerability
Speedy shoes to run far from uncomfortable situations

Not specific enough? Maybe the weapons people wield look more like cell phones to ward off public conversations, full schedules to keep from connecting and relationships, credit cards to solve problems temporarily, or fake smiles to cover hurt or indignation. Maybe weapons like those. We've seen them. We've used them.

These weapons are, again, deceptively protective. And really only somewhat effective against other people, definitely not for the long term. But when facing off against the real Enemy, there's a whole different set of armor available for our use.

Stand firm then, with the belt of truth buckled around your waist,
with the breastplate of righteousness in place, and with your feet
fitted with the readiness that comes from the gospel of peace. In
addition to all this, take up the shield of faith, with which you can
extinguish all the flaming arrows of the evil one. Take the helmet
of salvation and the sword of the Spirit, which is the word of God.
(Eph. 6:14–17)

This armor is for taking action, going on the defensive, striking back against the real Enemy, and standing firm. And it's fueled by God's power, not our own ability. As verse 10 in the same chapter says, "Be strong *in the Lord* and in *his* mighty power."

This armor is not, however, intended for self-protection. It isn't meant to keep out the hurt, frustration, and various other emotions that come into play when other people are involved. We will wound each other. Vulnerability opens us up to it. But I believe we can overcome so many of the things that keep us divided and instead find common ground.

When it comes to how we approach other people, Paul lays out a much different ensemble for us:

> As God's chosen people, holy and dearly loved, clothe yourselves with compassion, kindness, humility, gentleness and patience. Bear with each other and forgive one another if any of you has a grievance against someone. Forgive as the Lord forgave you. And over all these virtues put on love, which binds them all together in perfect unity. (Col. 3:12–14)

Defenses and weapons are not the solution with people. Instead, the garments in our spiritual closets are made of caring deeply for other people (see chapter 4), considering ourselves less, releasing our need to be the most important or always right, choosing to approach others with sympathy and restraint, and giving space for mistakes and misunderstandings. All in all, garments made of love.

An insightful quote sometimes attributed to activist and author Maya Angelou says, "I've learned that people will forget what you said, people will forget what you did, but people will never forget how you made them feel." What kind of atmosphere are you cultivating around yourself that will make you a safe space for stories to be told and for people to be themselves?

Defenses and weapons are not the solution with people. Instead, the garments in our spiritual closets are made of caring deeply for other people.

Discernment Disclaimer

An extra note here, because it's important: while we clothe ourselves in garments of love, we will always need to use Spirit-led discernment when it comes to other people, both in how we open up to them and what we allow from them.

Even though people are not our enemies, Satan can manipulate people in a number of ways to cause unnecessary destruction in one another's lives. There's a difference between a superficial cut and a mortal wound. There are occasional bumps and bruises and misunderstandings that come up in relationships, and then on the other hand, there is ongoing abuse and trauma.

We'll talk about boundaries in the next chapter. For now, please remember that you are a person of incredible value to the One who made you. It is not spiritual or faithful to condone violence against your body, your heart, or your mind, nor is it anyone's job or right to inflict violence on you. Please remember that even while not everyone is worthy of how you open up to them and what you share, our feelings are always safe with the God who created us and cares immensely for us.

Let's Do This

Vulnerability is contagious, and we can pass it on by starting with our own self-awareness and willingness to practice it in appropriate spaces.

Look up "feeling words" (ones that are more specific and nuanced than *angry* or *happy*), and make a list. Start applying them regularly in conversation. Having the proper language for what's going on in your heart and practicing it will help grow vulnerability and can inspire it in others.

Work It Out

1. How have moments of vulnerability surprised you? Consider a time when someone unexpectedly opened up to you, or the response when you opened up to someone else. What impact did that have on you?

2. Take time to intentionally put on compassion, kindness, humility, gentleness, and patience today. What might this look like as a daily practice for you?

_____

_____

_____

_____

_____

_____

_____

_____

3. How can you encourage people this very week? Consider someone with whom you might not ordinarily get a lot of contact who may be in need.

_____

_____

_____

_____

_____

_____

_____

_____

Three truths I know about God

◆ _____

◆ _____

◆ _____

Three things I'm grateful for

◆ _____

◆ _____

◆ _____

Three steps I can take moving forward

◆ _____

◆ _____

◆ _____

Watch Video 7

Find the link on page 28.

Video Notes

Reflective Prayer

Prayer Requests

Praises

Chapter 8

The Woman Who Is Too Much

Slamming my car door a little too hard and turning my key a little too aggressively, I pulled out of the driveway a little too fast.

With tears pouring out, screaming with frustration, and using words I probably shouldn't repeat, I steered my car to who knows where. It was getting dark, and I was new to the area. This wasn't the most rational idea. But I desperately needed an escape.

It's too much, God.

Within a matter of weeks, early in 2020, a series of challenges and bad news had come streaming in. Cancer had returned to someone close to us, family members were considering big life changes, our immediate family was getting over sickness and had recently made a big move across the country, and a step toward my dream career had been foiled, which felt like a huge setback. (This was even before the worldwide upheaval of that year came into the picture.)

The chaos at the beginning of the year was what motivated this impromptu journey. After a while, my screams subsided into a pleading prayer to the only One who was with me right at that moment.

I don't know what to do, God. There's nothing I can do.

We've all experienced when life feels like too much. The pain, challenges, and sorrows of this fallen world are pretty much guaranteed, as we talked about in chapter 4. But when they all happen at once, life seems unbearable. It feels like a mess that is more than we can handle.

And then when it comes to other people, sometimes their problems appear too much or too messy to be able to love and serve them well. Possibly we even feel burdened by or bitter toward others and the obligation we feel to help when our own lives feel so full.

Suddenly, where your heart might formerly have been free to give generously, it now feels at odds with the people you want to give to. Internally, you feel conflicted about setting limits and gaining approval.

In my sinful nature, I can and have run from the red flags of a person going through messy circumstances—as if my own life hasn't been messy and as though people haven't shown up for me regardless.

Where is God when life gets complicated? How does he expect us to respond to the mess—either for us or for someone else?

Really, like all the struggles with others we identify in this book, this is a battle within. We feel torn between establishing boundaries and choosing self-denial, and our Enemy wants us somewhere in the murky middle: where boundaries are "too selfish" but self-denial demands absolutely everything from you—because that's what God wants … right?

When Self-Denial and Boundaries Are Blurry

Growing up, I could only read Jesus' words on self-denial one way: that we should say yes and give to the fullest extent to anyone who asks us:

Give to the one who asks you, and do not turn away from the one who wants to borrow from you. (Matt. 5:42)

He said to them all: "Whoever wants to be my disciple must deny themselves and take up their cross daily and follow me." (Luke 9:23)

My command is this: Love each other as I have loved you. Greater love has no one than this: to lay down one's life for one's friends. (John 15:12–13)

And then, as a bonus, the most guilt-inducing verse I can think of came from James 4:17: *"If anyone, then, knows the good they ought to do and doesn't do it, it is sin for them."*

Maybe you have known the weight of this perspective. It feels like sin every time you say no without a good excuse. You feel ashamed if you feel reluctant to give and will even majorly contort your schedule or resources to fill someone else's needs. Whatever they believe to be an emergency becomes yours too. Anxiety kicks in every time you need to make a decision about whether or not you can help—and what the consequences will be if you don't. You feel like the only one who is able to help.

All this might leave you feeling paranoid (*they're just being nice because they need something*), unappreciated (*no one notices*), disgruntled (*no one helps me like I help others*), or just plain overwhelmed.

After describing all this to my counselor once, I still remember the gentle response: *"Is that how Jesus lived?"*

It stopped me in my tracks. My impulsive response was "Yes, of course!" Right? He was always healing people! Always feeding people! Always teaching!

But the more you look at the above verses in context, the less shady condemnation they are throwing. And the more you look at Jesus' life on earth—what he prioritized, how he both interacted with and withdrew from people, his reliance on God, his yeses and nos—they didn't add up to a life without discernment, priorities, and decisive limits.

Jesus didn't heal every single person who was suffering, didn't feed every person who came to listen to him preach, didn't always give satisfactory answers, and didn't show up as an earthly king to throw off the ties of oppression, as people expected. He didn't rush to fulfill requests, didn't always answer a question directly, didn't necessarily affirm those who thought they were doing the right thing, and didn't feed the egos of those in power.

Jesus disappointed people. And here's the thing: It wasn't because he was selfish or mean or careless or lazy, as might be assumed (and can sometimes be the case) when people say no.

Jesus simply knew what was most important for his limited time on earth, and even he as the Son of God knew what was and wasn't his to do. If Jesus didn't spin all the plates to keep people happy, then perhaps that's not our mission, either.

We establish boundaries when we set clear limits on what we need and expect for ourselves and others and then follow up on those limits. Boundaries allow us to take ownership of what is within our power to do and release responsibility for what is not. Setting healthy boundaries means stewarding well the resources God has given us. Healthy boundaries set the parameters for healthy relationships.

Or, as therapist Nedra Glover Tawwab says in her bestselling guide to creating and honoring limits, *Set Boundaries, Find Peace*, "People don't know what you want. It's your job to make it clear. Clarity saves relationships."[1] She cites these six areas of boundaries: physical, sexual, intellectual, emotional, material, and time.[2]

This is, by far, the hardest chapter for me to write, because these lines still feel blurry. I can believe that the best way to love people is to make them happy, no matter the cost. There's something in me that resists the word *no* and hates leaving people displeased. With blurry boundaries, I've hurt people by setting up walls where they shouldn't have been, and hurt myself by leaving gaping holes where there could have been protection and even healing.

Let's look to Jesus and into the Scriptures to determine some clarity to help us as we approach finding balance in boundaries and self-denial, areas in which we can feel especially conflicted.

People-Pleasing Aside

In John 6, Jesus got dumped by a crowd of people who, less than twenty-four hours before, wanted him to be king.

Here's the recap: After seeing Jesus heal the sick and following him out of town, a crowd of five thousand people was treated to a huge meal that had been multiplied from a little boy's small lunch. After witnessing this, the rave reviews poured in: the crowd called him "the Prophet who is to come"(v. 14) and even planned to make him king by force.

But Jesus, instead of basking in the praise and signing on the dotted line for fame and fortune, retreated to the mountain. Alone. Not even his disciples went with him.

Overnight he performed one of his most famous miracles for only a few witnesses: walking on choppy water to meet the disciples in a boat—miles from shore. Meanwhile the crowd, still seeking out Jesus, chased him down by land to the other side of the lake.

Then Jesus did the least expected thing—again. He called all five thousand of them out for showing up just for the food. He challenged them to step up to the plate (not the dinner one) and actually take action to live out their faith in God. "I am the bread of life," Jesus declared. "Whoever comes to me will never go hungry, and whoever believes in me will never be thirsty. But as I told you, you have seen me and still you do not believe" (vv. 35–36).

At the end of this scene, he foreshadowed the practice of Communion, telling the people they needed to actually eat his body and drink his blood to truly live with the Father. And that's when their adoration turned to abandonment. All those people who were giant Jesus fans before felt frustrated and turned away. (Thankfully, the disciples stayed strong.)

How easy it would have been to give the people what they wanted! Keep them happy! Enjoy the praise and approval! Gain power and influence! It seems like an easy yes.

And yet, those things weren't Jesus' goals. He never lost sight of his purpose here: to seek and save the lost. Although he cared for people's well-being physically, mentally, and emotionally, his top priority was spiritual. Feeding the people again, performing miracles again, accepting the job as king—these weren't actually needed. And that didn't sit well with the crowd.

People's approval just feels so good. To go without it can bring questions and doubts about ourselves (even when Scripture and Spirit tell us we're doing the right thing).

On my podcast, *Called Into Being*, I spoke with a friend, author Amanda Anderson, on the topic of people-pleasing. She revealed a number of things that blew my mind, and this was one of them:

> I am not actually being kind and others-centered when I'm a people-pleaser. I am selfishly trying to regulate my own anxiety. I make my decisions to lower my anxiety about how you perceive me and whether or not you think I am good, and my own internal

judge of whether or not I am good or I am doing enough. And that is about me, not about kindness.[3]

Jesus didn't need to regulate anxiety in this way, because for him it was never about people's praise. The kindest, most loving thing he could do for others was to tell them the truth.

It is necessary for us to disentangle our people-pleasing and need for approval from the concept of serving God and others. Perhaps our greatest way of taking on the kind of self-denial Jesus lived out for us is by removing our self-interest and self-doubt when it comes to other people.

What did Jesus do instead? He got time alone in the mountains. (Although it isn't stated, one could assume he was connecting with his Father in prayer, as was his practice when he was alone.) He performed a miracle only his closest friends could see instead of doing it for the benefit of the hungry crowd. He spoke clearly and directly to those who came after him, choosing truth over telling them what they wanted to hear.

Let's take our practicals from Jesus in this area:

- Deeply engage in a practice of prayer for God's wisdom and discernment in our callings.
- Find ways to give to others that go unseen and unapplauded—except by the God who sees everything.
- Communicate boundaries clearly instead of avoiding the conflict.

May we continue to surrender our people-pleasing and approval-seeking to the Father and find satisfaction in pleasing and being approved by him.

Keep in Step with the Spirit

A large part of being able to set healthy boundaries in your life is knowing the difference between what you can and can't do. And I don't know about you, but usually my ego is inflated when it comes to my abilities and control.

When someone asks for help, my thinking immediately goes like this: *I should be able to do that. I have what I need. I am resourceful enough to get it all done. I'm capable on my own.* The other extreme to this thinking would be: *I couldn't possibly. That would never work. Who has the time? I'm not equipped.* Note the absence of God from either thought process (as warned about in Ps. 10:4).

Discernment comes into play here. It may be a good thing to help someone else. But is it the best thing? The right thing? The answer is true wisdom direct from the source (see Prov. 2:6–11; James 1:5).

A beautiful image of this is in Galatians 5:25, which says, "Since we live by the Spirit, let us keep in step with the Spirit." *The Message* puts the same passage this way: "Let us make sure that we do not just hold it as an idea in our heads or a sentiment in our hearts, but work out its implications in every detail of our lives."

The Spirit isn't the backup plan when all else fails. God gifted the Spirit as our direct line to him, a living helper so we can know him intimately and understand his divine perspective (see 1 Cor. 2:11–12). Jesus' disciples are meant to have Spirit-centered lives, which happens through the practices of reading God's Word, praying constantly, seeking advice from trusted advisors, and honestly just making the time to listen and pay attention instead of instantly reacting.

The Spirit isn't the backup plan when all else fails.

The result of living Spirit-led? It comes in the verses just before "keep in step with the Spirit," in Galatians 5:22–24:

> The fruit of the Spirit is love, joy, peace, forbearance, kindness, goodness, faithfulness, gentleness and self-control. Against such things there is no law. Those who belong to Christ Jesus have crucified the flesh with its passions and desires.

A Spirit-led life leads us to good fruit and, I believe, even the balance that we can find so elusive.

Steward Your Responsibilities Well

A passage that tends to get a lot of reference when it comes to boundaries is this one:

> *Carry each other's burdens*, and in this way you will fulfill the law of Christ.... Each one should test their own actions. Then they can take pride in themselves alone, without comparing themselves to someone else, for *each one should carry their own load*. (Gal. 6:2, 4–5)

How does it play out to both "carry each other's burdens" to "fulfill the law of Christ" while also maintaining that "each one should carry their own load"? Don't those two contradict? The original Greek words carry a deeper meaning.

The word translated as "burden" in verse 2, which is βάρη (*barē*), means "heaviness, weight, burden, or trouble," according to *Thayer's Greek Lexicon*.[4] In an article from the website Answers in Genesis, Scot Chadwick connects this word to its other uses in Scripture, finding that this word related to "situations in life that are weighty and oppressive,"[5] like overwhelming physical conditions and also temptations to sin. These kinds of moments of physical and emotional overwhelm are opportunities to love one another with compassion and support. Verse 1 in the chapter suggests that these situations can lead to finding ourselves in sinful traps, requiring gentle restoration; verse 3 is a reminder that you yourself may need this kind of compassion and support someday.

But then the word translated as "load" in verse 5 is φορτίον (*phortion*). The only other use of this word in the New Testament is in Matthew 11:30, where it says, "My *burden* is light." This type of load is talking about responsibilities that are meant to be individual.[6] These are the responsibilities entrusted to our care as well as the decisions made by us that we will answer to God for someday.[7]

Simply put, some responsibilities are ours to carry individually (but become lighter with Jesus!), and some burdens are those we can help one another shoulder. Chapter 4 talks about developing compassion and what it might look like to support someone in crisis, so I won't go any further into that here. But individual responsibilities? Let's talk.

Think back to the passage in Matthew 25 about the servants and the bags of gold. The master was generous in what he offered yet still expected an answer for what he'd given them when he returned. "Well done, good and faithful servant!" he said to the two who showed a return on his investment. "You have been faithful with a few things; I will put you in charge of many things. Come and share your master's happiness!" (v. 23).

What sorts of things has God given us as our own responsibilities, ones we will answer for someday?

Our actions
Our thoughts
Our feelings
Our words

Our decisions and their consequences

Our spiritual, physical, mental, and emotional well-being

Our mistakes

Our needs and desires

What we allow in our lives and agree to

The people who depend on us for their basic needs, attention, and
     love (like our children or dependent family members)

Here are things we can't control, things that fall outside of our responsibility:

The feelings of others

The thoughts of others

The behavior and actions of others

The opinions of others

The mistakes of others

The decisions of others and their consequences

The character growth and development of others

The commitments and agreements of other people

On a surface level, it might feel good to take care of problems for someone else. But taking over their responsibilities means less of an opportunity for them to address their own. And such action often leaves you neglecting yours. Often, others come to rely on the one who always comes in and saves the day.

Perhaps that's what Jesus was intending to get across in the sixth chapter of John. The more he provided for people, the easier it became to support and applaud him. But his goal was actually helping them to believe and follow him, the best for them (and for us), lasting beyond his time on earth.

Serve to Your Strengths

One of my best friends, Cheryl, shared something she's been learning that fits all these areas: *serve to your strengths*. Sometimes we rally ourselves to take on tasks because of people-pleasing, or because the help seems very needed, or because it feels good to be asked to take on a certain role, even if it's not quite in our wheelhouse. And then we burn out fast because it's just not what we were meant to do in this season (or ever). As she shared, I could absolutely relate.

Sadly, this can be part of church culture. There can be pressure to serve in certain areas just because it's needed and you're spiritually mature. There can be a big emphasis on being a leader, joining mission teams, interning, or doing "big things for God." Sometimes you get "voluntold" as opposed to volunteering. This is where discernment comes into play: praying, seeking advice, remaining humble. (And trusting that the one asking you is doing the same.)

When we say no, we make room for people who actually have that talent to step up. And saying no leaves us open to take on one of the many needs of the church that might go unseen, maybe because it isn't front and center.

Or perhaps you say yes, at least for a season, and discover a skill you didn't know you had. Leave room to reevaluate and know that seasons change.

And if you're not serving the church in some way—what's your hesitation? God has a plan for you here in his kingdom, as we've been discussing throughout this book. What part of the body are you (1 Cor. 12)? What good works are you living out (Eph. 2:10)?

Sometimes life is messy and it isn't your season to serve. But if it's *never* your season to serve, that's a bit of a red flag. The church has so many needs, so many incredible ways to serve. There's something for everyone. We cannot take ourselves out of the running to give.

Let People Love You

One night our friends invited us over for dinner. Well, just my two kids and me. Our family was going through a particularly rough season when my husband had to travel out of town every week for days at a time. Meanwhile, my youngest was going through a really hard time at school, which I was trying to navigate on my own between morning and bedtime routines, household chores, and soccer games. Honestly, I felt at my breaking point.

Solo parents are absolute superheroes, by the way.

"What can I bring?" I asked earlier that day, trying to calculate when I could slip in a quick trip to the store. "Just yourselves," my friend Lauren assured me, and I took her up on it.

We arrived. Her husband took all our kids into the next room to eat and watch a movie, and I was able to relax with my friend, pouring out my troubles and filling up both physically and emotionally.

It felt awkward to be so generously served without really being able to give anything back. And yet it was just what was needed. I felt entirely grateful, bolstered for another week ahead.

It is an obvious boundary issue to let people dictate your behavior and constantly say yes to those who ask without discernment. It is also a boundary issue, although perhaps less obvious, to not let anyone in. *"No, I don't need help. No, I've got this. No, I could never accept that."* (See chapter 6.)

God's plan for us is community, connection, and collaboration. It's also God's plan to bring us comfort—not only that, but to work through us to provide relief for others.

> Praise be to the God and Father of our Lord Jesus Christ, the Father
> of compassion and the God of all comfort, who comforts us in all

our troubles, so that we can comfort those in any trouble with the comfort we ourselves receive from God. (2 Cor. 1:3–4)

I used to feel equally awkward about gifts people bought for us, whether for our wedding or the babies that came later. What came with the gifts was a nagging feeling of having to return the favor, even though it would have been impossible to match everyone's generosity.

God's plan for us is community, connection, and collaboration.

But this is how it works: we're all simply taking turns practicing generosity. You receive the kindness of others, and then when you're able, you pass it on. Just as those who came before me offered gifts, encouragement, meals, and advice, when it's my turn, I can do the same for someone else in that position.

It's okay to let people love and help you. Sometimes in the moment, you don't have anything left to give in return. And yet as your comfort grows, it's something you can continue to pass on. As Galatians 6:2 says, again, "in this way you will fulfill the law of Christ." And as we each fulfill Christ's law, we pass on kindness and generosity in growing measure that affect our circles, communities, and beyond.

Accept Other People's Boundaries

Last but not least important is this: the one who wants to be able to give a no and leave it at that has to also respect others enough to let them do the same.

We don't have to understand their boundaries. We don't have to ask if they've done the heart work or prayed about it or to give us more information.

And that is *hard* sometimes. Assumptions, judgment, and shame are difficult habits to break, usually because they're contagious—what we experience from other people gets passed on.

> *Why won't you help me? I helped you!*
> *Surely you don't have anything better going on.*
> *You're just being selfish.*
> *Well, what would Jesus do?*
> *… (rolls their eyes) …*
> *… (radio silence) …*

Have I thought, said, or done these things, or even worse things? It's likely. Has someone thought, said, or done these to me, or worse? Also likely. We're not perfect.

But it's vital that we grow toward accepting the limits of others, just as God extends loving limits to us and allows us to set limits with others. Lord, help us with this! And when we fail, help us to be conscious enough to apologize and try again.

God's love for us is without limit, but he also loves us enough to show us limits. The clearer we get in our own boundaries with others, the more we can understand what God has set in place for us: "The boundary lines have fallen for me in pleasant places; surely I have a delightful inheritance" (Ps. 16:6).

Let's Do This

Take some time to sit down and assess your boundaries in these six areas: physical, sexual, intellectual, emotional, material, and time. Consider what feels honoring to you and what feels violating, and set two clear and appropriate boundaries for each area. For example, for time boundaries: "I will not drop my responsibility last minute to help you with yours." Or set a boundary for yourself that may affect others, like turning off your phone for certain hours of the day while you're working or focused on family.

Work It Out

1. Read John 6. What surprises you the most about Jesus' interactions? Which of the three practical steps Jesus shows in this chapter can you take to battle people-pleasing?

_____

_____

_____

_____

_____

_____

_____

_____

_____

_____

_____

_____

_____

_____

_____

_____

_____

_____

_____

_____

2. What does it look like for you to "keep in step with the Spirit"? What practices help you remain Spirit-centered?

3. What is a way that you are able to provide for someone else in their time of need? What is a way that you can let someone else serve you in yours?

Three truths I know about God

✦ _____
  _____

✦ _____
  _____

✦ _____
  _____

Three things I'm grateful for

✦ _____
  _____

✦ _____
  _____

✦ _____
  _____

Three steps I can take moving forward

✦ _____
  _____

✦ _____
  _____

✦ _____
  _____

Watch Video 8

Find the link on page 28.

Video Notes

Reflective Prayer

Prayer Requests

Praises

Chapter 9

The Woman in the Mirror

Remember in the last chapter when I shared about a period of my life when my struggles felt too big for me to handle? Let's finish that story.

You see, just after I hit my total emotional breaking point, on a late-night drive that probably wasn't a great idea, the car slowed to a stop at a red light, and I ended my prayer with a whisper. *"I have nothing, God. What do you want from me? There's nothing much I can offer."*

And then, as clearly if they were said aloud, words came to mind that didn't come from me:

I do my best work with nothing.

Whoa. The more I contemplated this thought, feeling it out like a smooth stone in my palm, the more I realized how true this statement was.

Yes—yes, you do, Lord.

Time and time again he has proven it. He is the one who parted the sea when the Israelites were trapped between drowning and being dragged back to oppression. He multiplied a child's lunch to feed a whole crowd of adults and children. He helped barren women conceive and give birth. He brought people back from the dead, literally and figuratively. He transformed those who were despised or unimpressive or scared or incapable into those with a mission, an army, a church, or a movement. From nothing, he called into being the sun and stars and plants and animals and people. And on and on and on.

Where everything appears hopeless and impossible for people, God steps up and rolls up his sleeves.

So, my nothing much? It doesn't do anything to hinder the miracles he can do. Not because of me. Because of him.

> *Where everything appears hopeless and impossible for people, God steps up and rolls up his sleeves.*

That concept stuck with me through that year (2020, need I remind you) and beyond. But as often happens, an insecurity crept in, a long-standing one that was something else to examine and consider:

> If I have nothing much to offer, does that mean I *am* nothing much?

A Hard Look in the Mirror

The woman I've been most judgmental and condescending toward during much of my life has been the one in the mirror. She was never good enough, pretty enough, smart enough, or talented enough. She was the odd one out, the one who didn't belong (only she was too naive to realize it). I was so hateful toward her that even when trusted friends said kind things about her, I truly believed they were lying just to be nice.

Recently one of my best friends posted a bunch of photos from years of summer camp we both grew up attending. Looking at those photos and finding a younger me, it all came back—how much burden I put on that girl to be perfect. How much she so relied on people's approval for her confidence. How many times I had said her body wasn't shaped right, her face too angular, her chin too big, her hair too boring, her nose too crooked. But now all I could see in these pictures was a beautiful girl, in her element, completely unworthy of the criticism I'd heaped on her.

Even five or so years ago, I would have answered the question above with a resounding yes. *You are nothing. You are worthless. The only thing redeemable about you is that Jesus died for you.*

But I would have been wrong. The true, joy-filled answer is no. "Nothing much" is our posture, not our identity. We'll get back to the posture part in a little bit. But the identity God gave us is this: Beloved. Wanted. Accepted.

We are enough in him and for him. When we get this concept straight, everything else follows.

"I am enough" is one of those tricky terms in Christian circles. We can take it pridefully, soaking up society's standards of self-reliance and "pulling yourself up by your bootstraps." Sometimes to avoid this, we go to the other extreme: "I am worthless and useless."

Only God can take us to the middle ground between these two extremes. Because of God, I am worthy and loved. Because of God, the possibilities are endless.

We've already been through so many truths in this book. But sometimes the biggest battle is within ourselves. If you need an identity check, whether for the first time or as a reminder of who God says you are, let's look into some of the truths that allow us to have full confidence in him.

Not Condemned

A good courtroom drama always draws me in. Usually, the story line involves a struggle between a smooth-talking prosecutor and an honest defender: There comes an eventual airtight argument that wins over the judge and jury, granting justice to the one seeking it. There's a victorious swell of music, a cheering gallery of people, and a close-up of the teary-eyed defendant who gets to walk free.

The identity God gave us is this: Beloved. Wanted. Accepted.

Much as we would rather not be, we're all on trial in that defendant seat. We beg for mercy, although I think we all know what side of justice we really land on. And constantly, we have two dueling characters arguing over us.

Then I heard a loud voice in heaven say:

"Now have come the salvation and the power
    and the kingdom of our God,
    and the authority of his Messiah.
For the accuser of our brothers and sisters,
    who accuses them before our God day and night,
    has been hurled down." (Rev. 12:10)

The accuser, our Enemy, will find every single opportunity to point out our unworthiness, failures, and shame: "Did you see that? Her sin is consuming her. Here's the evidence: a bad attitude, judgmental thoughts, colorful language, passive aggression. Surely you can't allow someone like *that* into your presence. She's supposed to be representing you, but she makes you look *terrible*. Time to give up on her already."

> My dear children, I write this to you so that you will not sin. But
> if anybody does sin, we have an advocate with the Father—Jesus
> Christ, the Righteous One. (1 John 2:1)

Meanwhile, our constant advocate, Jesus, goes toe to toe with the accuser: "Lord, forgive her. She doesn't know what she's doing. I've been there and experienced what she is going through. No, she shouldn't have made those choices. But remember how much you love her, how far you are willing to go for her, why she is precious and unique to you. If there's anyone to punish, let me take the blame. Let her go free."

Which voice is the loudest in your head? Chances are, with the woman in the mirror as the enemy, the accuser's words sound the most familiar. But let's not confuse their sources. One voice belongs to the real Enemy. The other belongs to the Savior, who is the "the exact representation of [God's] being" (Heb. 1:3). He physically represents God's heart toward us. And he is on our side.

We are operating under a brand-new set of laws, one that knocks our worldly legal system out of the water. As Romans 8:1–2 declares, "There is now *no condemnation* for those who are in Christ Jesus, because through Christ Jesus the law of the Spirit who gives life has set you free from the law of sin and death."

It's time to call the condemnation what it is and release it. Let go of the harmful self-talk and brutal self-assessments. Those words that are dripping with shame, punishment, hatred, accusation? Those are not from God. They're not from Jesus. And they don't win. This is why we continue to affirm ourselves with the solid truth of the Word of God.

Chosen

When you're a chronic people-pleaser, being chosen is the best feeling. Every time I was picked for a position at school, asked to lead a group, handed an invitation, or called back for a second job interview, I felt a little puffed up. Someone chose *me*.

But then again, every rejection feels like a crushing blow, spiraling into thoughts of *Why not me? What's wrong with me?* I round up my resources, attempting to be even more "chooseable" and less "rejectable" next time.

It's time to call the condemnation what it is and release it. Let go of the harmful self-talk and brutal self-assessments.

We hang our hats on the fickle opinions of other people. We spin our wheels making ourselves agreeable and likable, yet we end up stumped (and exhausted) when we're not picked.

All this is beside the point that as believers, we have already been exclusively selected by the only One whose opinion actually matters. (And if you're not sure yet about being a believer, don't automatically assume you're excluded. You are still called. Perhaps this book is only one step in your journey. What you do with the call is up to you.)

Why care about God's opinion and not that of other people? Because he is unconditionally faithful and loving. He doesn't judge people based on results or resumes. He designed you and knows you better than anyone. He's proven his love for you by sacrificing what he holds most dear. And at the end of the day, he holds the authority over this world and everything in it.

Do you know of a single human being who can make all of those claims? I can count them on no hands. And this is the One who says he has specially picked you:

> In him we were also chosen, having been predestined according to the plan of him who works out everything in conformity with the purpose of his will, in order that we, who were the first to put our hope in Christ, might be for the praise of his glory. (Eph. 1:11–12)

> We know, brothers and sisters loved by God, that he has chosen you, because our gospel came to you not simply with words but also with power, with the Holy Spirit and deep conviction. (1 Thess. 1:4–5a)

> You are a chosen people, a royal priesthood, a holy nation, God's special possession, that you may declare the praises of him who called you out of darkness into his wonderful light. (1 Pet. 2:9)

Let's not find our worth and identity in the people of this world, who are just as temporary and fickle as we are. Let's put these crucial questions in the hands of our God, who has hand-selected and included us.

Adopted

One of the dearest little girls in my life was adopted as a toddler from China. When a best friend and her husband were matched with this child, they had some understandable hesitation at first. She had developmental delays, including communication and mobility. There was no way to know the full extent of her medical conditions, nor how she would fare in the future. And yet they couldn't deny the sense that this little girl was the one—the missing piece for their family.

Because of their unwavering faith and support, Lizzie, as they called her, has come such a long way. When we met, she wasn't able to even say hello. She now recognizes me as her "auntie," smiles, says hi, blows kisses, and interacts. This little girl, who couldn't stand unassisted or walk when her parents met her, now runs with joy. Where there were no words, now she can communicate. This girl can look at books for hours. Have a baby or a dog? She will not leave your side.

If you ask her mom, she will say that Lizzie was always meant to be her daughter. And there's no doubt or question about it. It hasn't been an easy road. But their family wouldn't have it any other way.

That is the happiest ending: to find a place of belonging, be welcomed home, and find your forever family. Now, can you wrap your mind around the magnitude of God welcoming us into his home as full sons and daughters? God looked at you and said, "I want her in my family. Not temporarily, not with conditions, but fully and completely. Every bit my daughter as my Son." Why? Purely because he loves and delights in you.

> The Spirit you received does not make you slaves, so that you live in fear again; rather, the Spirit you received brought about your adoption to sonship. And by him we cry, "*Abba*, Father." (Rom. 8:15)

> When the set time had fully come, God sent his Son, born of a woman, born under the law, to redeem those under the law, that we might receive adoption to sonship. Because you are his sons, God sent the Spirit of his Son into our hearts, the Spirit who calls out, "*Abba*, Father." So you are no longer a slave, but

God's child; and since you are his child, God has made you also an heir. (Gal. 4:4–7)

The word *heir* is used multiple times in reference to our adoption by God. It establishes the point that we aren't just a secondary part of God's household, like servants. This is permanent, with no strings. We can't lose our place, as Jesus says in John 8:34–36. We have a share in the inheritance, just like Christ if we live as he did (see Rom. 8:17).

You're in. You're part of the family. You belong here.

Purposed and Equipped

In the movie *Hugo* (based on the book *The Invention of Hugo Cabret* by Brian Selznick), a mysterious boy named Hugo hides in the walls of a Parisian train station, trying not to get caught by the station inspector. As you watch the movie, you get a sense of his lostness: he's alone, without a family, living in the moment, and unable to see past his day-to-day survival.

At one point in the movie, he speaks to his new friend, Isabelle, as they look out over the city from the clock tower.

"I'd imagine the whole world was one big machine," he observed. "Machines never come with any extra parts, you know. They always come with the exact amount they need. So I figured, if the entire world was one big machine, I couldn't be an extra part. I had to be here for some reason. And that means you have to be here for some reason too."[1]

If you've ever felt like an extra part, these words might resonate with you as they did for me. Funny enough, God says something similar, and his words resonate in an even greater way:

You are the body of Christ, and each one of you is a part of it. (1 Cor. 12:27)

> We are God's handiwork, created in Christ Jesus to do good
> works, which God prepared in advance for us to do. (Eph. 2:10)

> Being confident of this, that he who began a good work in you will
> carry it on to completion until the day of Christ Jesus. (Phil. 1:6)

God isn't unintentional with us. He's not waiting around to see if he needs us as a backup, just in case his first choice doesn't work out. You—yes, *you*—have purpose. Not only that, but God is growing you and working through you to bring you up to the task. And he gives us everything we need to be equipped for whatever job he has for us: 2 Timothy 3:16–17 and 2 Peter 1:3–4 promise God's provision for the assignments he has for us.

I love the whole message of 1 Corinthians 12, especially as it relates to this book and especially this chapter, because it emphasizes the fact that we all have different jobs and tasks to which God calls us. We can't say we're too good for anyone else or not good enough to be included. God has given us our assignments, and they are all part of the bigger plan.

Wildly Confident and Realistically Humble

With God as our architect and Jesus as our foundation, we can take on confidence like we've only dreamed of in our most insecure moments. Not based on our own changing talents or qualities or accolades but based on an unchanging God and a high priest who intervenes for us forever:

> Friends, we can now—without hesitation—walk right up to God,
> into "the Holy Place." Jesus has cleared the way by the blood of his
> sacrifice, acting as our priest before God. The "curtain" into God's
> presence is his body.

So let's *do* it—full of belief, confident that we're presentable inside and out. Let's keep a firm grip on the promises that keep us going. He always keeps his word. (Heb. 10:19–23 MSG)

Hebrews 4:15–16 (as we've already talked about) says something similar: "We do not have a high priest who is unable to empathize with our weaknesses, but we have one who has been tempted in every way, just as we are—yet he did not sin. Let us then approach God's throne of grace with confidence, so that we may receive mercy and find grace to help us in our time of need."

Did you catch these distinctions: Our weaknesses that Jesus can empathize with? Our constant seeking of mercy and grace? Our "time of need"?

God knows his reader here. He recognizes and acknowledges what we lack. It doesn't present any barrier to our getting to be with and know him. But it *exists*.

This takes us back to our initial assessment: the phrase "nothing much" is our posture, not our identity. It's an attitude we choose to adopt out of the humble awareness of the truth: we are not capable on our own, so we can give up our futile attempts to prove ourselves. As we've seen, the reasons for our confidence are established. But we accept our limitations and shortcomings.

Jesus himself sets the example:

Have the same mindset as Christ Jesus:

Who, being in very nature God,
    did not consider equality with God something to be used to
    his own advantage;
rather, he made himself nothing
    by taking the very nature of a servant,
    being made in human likeness.

And being found in appearance as a man,

   he humbled himself

   by becoming obedient to death—

   even death on a cross! (Phil. 2:5–8)

No one would dare say that Jesus was nothing much. Even a world that doesn't necessarily believe in his divinity can see the influence he had. For those of us who truly know him, we realize he was equal to and had access to the same power as God (although we ourselves cannot make those claims). And yet verse 7 tells us, "He made himself nothing." It was this posture he opted for, submitting himself to God, obeying his plan, and accepting the limitations of being human (without sinning).

Hebrews 5:8–10 says that Jesus, like us, "learned obedience from what he suffered and, once made perfect, he became the source of eternal salvation for all who obey him and was designated by God to be high priest in the order of Melchizedek."

Because of his humble posture, he suffered and obeyed and was made perfect, all in order to achieve our salvation. Yet at the same time, he was confident and assured in this world, not held back by the fickle opinions of people. (Reread John 2:24–25.) He knew who he was to God and his purpose here on earth. Nothing, not even Satan himself, could shake that.

Good news: You can have the very same confidence in God's identity for *you*. God looks at us with love, having tenderly and intentionally crafted our characters and embodied selves. He looks at us with hope, knowing all the possibilities and potential for how he can use us for his glory, despite our lack, because he can work through us. And as believers, because of Jesus who removes our sin from the picture, he sees us as wholly redeemed and made new.

From Written Words to Lived Word

In what practical ways can you go from feeling lost in insecurity and inadequacy to finding wild confidence in what God says about you?

Stop those thoughts in their tracks. Call them what they are—harmful, negative, shaming, condemning. Attribute them to their true source: Satan.

Do your homework. Dig through Scriptures and find the ones God says about you. Write them down. Meditate on them. Hold on to them.

Test the Scriptures. It's one thing for me to tell you God says nice things about you. It's another to feel their power in real life. So apply them to your situation—see if your thoughts align with what Scripture actually says. Or, if the Scriptures feel too good to be true, talk them out with a friend, read multiple versions, find cross-references, seek out a commentary or study. Go more than surface deep.

Be transformed. Romans 12:2a says, "Do not conform to the pattern of this world, but be transformed by the renewing of your mind." Don't take on the world's depreciation, whether toward yourself or others. Little by little, the ways you fight for victory over the lies add up. We are taking back our minds and choosing truth.

Walk humbly. Realize your limitations and remain in Jesus. Bring your burdens, worries, and plans to God, and offer them up to him. Listen for his words by searching out the Scriptures and paying attention to the Spirit's promptings. Through prayer, align your heart with his and ask for discernment in the choices you make.

This is something we partner in with God, by the way. We commit to continually showing up and remaining with him, and he works with us to bring about transformation.

How long does this take? Well, remember how I used to believe people complimenting me were actually lying? Yeah, it took awhile to not only believe their words but also God's words.

There's a scientific word for this: *neuroplasticity*, the fact that the brain is malleable and sometimes needs help strengthening its resilience to face struggles with positivity and courage instead of responding out of negativity and fear.

God formed our brains to adapt to our circumstances. What we put in and allow are connections in our brains that become stronger with time. Where are your thoughts? Do you allow them to rule you based on your emotions, or do you keep them in check with the truth of God's Word?

The woman in the mirror doesn't need to be an enemy. With time and intention, we can find the identity, worth, and confidence that God so freely offers us.

Let's Do This

Take a few minutes to honestly journal the negative things you believe about yourself. Take a few minutes to process them. (If you're like me, it may feel painful to think about and write out these thoughts.) Then go back and address those lies one by one, with Scripture, if possible. Ask yourself, "Is that what God really says about me?" For example, one lie I wrote down was a belief that God wanted me to fail and be humiliated. Psalm 3:1-6 addressed this lie and helped me feel strengthened and confident that God lifts my head and fights for me.

Work It Out

1. Which of the promises resonates the most with you in this season: not condemned, chosen, adopted, purposed, or equipped?

2. What traits does God have that make him the most trustworthy being in which to rest your confidence?

3. What will it look like for you to step out in wild confidence? How can you remain in God humbly at the same time?

Three truths I know about God

Three things I'm grateful for

Three steps I can take moving forward

Watch Video 9

Find the link on page 28.

Video Notes

Reflective Prayer

Prayer Requests

Praises

Embrace the Ongoing Process

At the playground, the feelings washed over me again.

It was just a "welcome to school" playdate: totally low-pressure, with all of us parents in the same boat of meeting new people and learning the ropes before our children started school. But it felt more like walking right back into the high school cafeteria, self-conscious of my outfit and hair and anxiously searching for someone to sit with.

Even though we were one of the first families there, finding the right place to park ourselves felt like a monumental test. After a few minutes of getting the kids settled and noticing a couple of parents milling around, I finally struck up a conversation with a mom sitting by herself.

Soon a small group of us had gathered, and we were all chatting fairly easily. Another mom came up and sat near us but didn't join the group. It occurred to me that I should invite her in, knowing full well how uncomfortable it feels to break into the conversation. But then a sudden, surprising inkling of power came over me. *I'm already midconversation, already part of this. If she wants to jump in, she can. Why should I work harder to include her?*

Even as these thoughts raced through my brain, I knew they were ridiculously selfish and arrogant. A much more considerate mom hopped in and included the woman with the group. (Eventually I got the chance to repent and talk with her.)

Between chatting and moments of pause, I found myself observing and weighing out the differences between my kids and me, and the other moms and their children. The encounter went from judging appearances (*she obviously dressed to impress … I wonder if people noticed I put on makeup today*) to behavior (*someone is a little overly friendly … wait, no one is talking to me anymore … what's wrong with me?*). At times I felt puffed up with how well my children were behaving; the next I was running, embarrassed, to break up a fight between my two.

Who's writing a book on comparison and competition? Oh yeah … *me*! (Face, meet palm.)

This is the imperfect journey, and we're all smack in the middle. It's not a finish line you cross or a goal you achieve and then move on to something else. No one can walk this road without stumbling or veering off course.

Or as *The Passion Translation* paraphrases Paul's words in Philippians 3:12: "I admit that I haven't yet acquired the absolute fullness that I'm pursuing, but I run with passion *into his abundance* so that I may reach the purpose for which Christ Jesus laid hold of me to make me his own."

Our souls long for the abundant life that doesn't depend on competing with people around us, falling and rising factors, and temporary treasure. And the good news? It's right there waiting for you. You just have to keep returning to God's character and his identity for you. That's where your security lies. (See chapter 9.)

Building Up the Kingdom

In the introduction, I talked about how comparison is something we do naturally. It's how we determine our roles and how we fit in and belong as we seek to fill core human needs. Society has told us that our problems stem from comparison and to simply get rid of it. But to get rid of the instinct is kind of impossible.

If comparison is part of life, you know what that tells me? That people are meant to consider our place in the world. Only it's not to figure out how we can win and come out on top. It's to figure out what we have to contribute. If that's the case, differences are advantages, not threats.

No, it's to find out how we fit together, like puzzle pieces. She's playing her part. Her gifts and skills call me higher. Where I can't, maybe she can. And vice versa.

It also indicates that our value can't be derived from our roles and achievements and talents as compared to other people. Because if it could, it would ebb and flow daily. There must be another standard for our worth—and there is.

I like how Paul lays it all out in 1 Corinthians 12. He wasn't interested in the arguing, artificial humility, or acts of bravado. The important thing was building up the kingdom of God, and everyone had a part to play in that. Those points are still true today.

> There are different kinds of gifts, but the same Spirit distributes them. There are different kinds of service, but the same Lord. There are different kinds of working, but in all of them and in everyone it is the same God at work.
>
> Now to each one the manifestation of the Spirit is given for the common good. (1 Cor. 12:4–7)

As we take ourselves out of the rat race, can we take a moment to just consider the generosity of God? He has a plan, and he's made small, lowly people part of it. He abundantly gives good gifts, because what else would we have to contribute? It's all about him from beginning to end. It's all to him (drawing ourselves nearer), through him (by his power), and for him (for his glory).

Back to Paul's declaration in 1 Corinthians 12, but in Eugene Peterson's paraphrase (I think Paul would have approved): "I want you to think about how all this makes you more significant, not less. A body isn't just a single part blown up into something huge. It's all the different-but-similar parts arranged and functioning together" (v. 14).

And then in verses 19–20 here's what we discover: "But I also want you to think about how this keeps your significance from getting blown up into self-importance. For no matter how significant you are, it is only because of what you are a *part* of" (MSG).

> *He has a plan, and he's made small, lowly people part of it.*

As mentioned in the last chapter, both confidence and humility come with this. *Both–and.* The confidence that God loves us, chose us, identifies us, and has purpose for us. It's the humble acceptance of what we're part of (building up his kingdom) and our identity in God that makes us significant. It all functions together, and it all is part of one beautiful design.

The more we can let go of self-importance and insecurity, the more we can focus on the community and the mission. Let us choose contentment, compassion, community, courage, and conviction over competition.

Creating a Culture of Community

While working to relax our culture of scarcity and stinginess, we can focus on a few practical ways to cultivate community rather than relying on self-protection and defense. We can make such an incredible impact for working together and building the kingdom if we set aside some of our insecurities and self-doubt. Where can we start?

Be Quick to Assume Good Intentions

What comes of being quick to judge and assume and compete is an attitude of cynicism and bitterness that is hard to overcome. And that's all without necessarily knowing what the other person is thinking! Instead, ask questions and take on a generous spirit. Maybe there is more going on than you know. Remember that people are all *imago dei*: made in the image of God.

Speak Life and Light to Others

Why does it feel socially unacceptable to give out compliments and endearments? It feels uncomfortable to tell someone you care about them, recognize their hard work verbally, or say something kind and affirming about what they're going through. And yet what a difference it makes in the lives of others! It might be just what they needed to hear.

Listen to the Spirit's Prompting

When you don't know what to say or do, the Spirit is able to intervene. The Spirit gives us nudges in the right direction, even if that guidance feels like something that doesn't come naturally to us. That might happen with words (see above) or even actions, to do something that will benefit someone else. Remember, the ruler of this world is our Enemy, and he generates a society that makes kindness and generosity uncomfortable and inaccessible. Trust the Spirit. The guidance will probably go contrary to what the world tells you, and maybe that's just what we need.

Let us choose contentment,

compassion, community, courage,

and conviction over competition.

Good for Her

Many people gravitate to TV shows and movies for comfort. There are a few actors I would consider common denominators in my comfort entertainment of choice, specifically people who never fail to make me laugh.

Amy Poehler is one of them. If you find me in tears or wallowing, just get me to a TV, load up *Parks and Recreation*, and press Play. (If you need a laugh, or multiple, I highly recommend season 3, episode 2, "Flu Season," or season 4, episode 4, "Pawnee Rangers.") So when I saw she wrote a book, *Yes Please*, I snatched it up. There was so much wisdom in there, but my favorite quote and piece of advice is this mantra: "Good for her! Not for me."[1]

How I interpret it is this: I can be happy for her and not take her success story as some kind of personal blow. I can celebrate good things for her and be confident in what God has for me. I can mourn with her and support her and still experience the good in my life. The two don't have to conflict.

This thought is just the appropriate mindset to wrap up this book and move forward into a newfound freedom from competition and feelings of inadequacy.

Good for her.

Good for her: pursuing her purpose.

Good for her: fighting for what she believes in.

Good for her: opening up.

Good for her: showing vulnerability.

Good for her: rocking her career.

Good for her: determining her boundaries.

Good for her: obeying God.

Good for her: sacrificing for her family.

Good for her: celebrating her wins.

Maybe those things are not for you right now. Or maybe they are things you might typically feel judgmental about, turned into compliments and encouragement for her. Find the good; cheer her on; keep going.

And then, separately, but with no less feeling:

Good for you.

Good for you: deciding that you will not waste any more time competing with other women for what wasn't meant for you.

Good for you: clearly identifying your true Enemy and being aware of his schemes.

Good for you: pursuing your own role in building the kingdom of God while supporting her in hers.

Good for you: planting your worth firmly in what God says about you and not in worldly metrics.

Good for you: choosing humility and gratitude over self-protection, envy, and selfish ambition.

Good for you: setting aside fear and competition to live out your own messy and imperfect faith.

Good for you. Friend, I'm rejoicing with you and cheering you on.

Reflections

Acknowledgments

This book has been a partnership with God and an adventure from beginning to end. There are so many ways this process did not happen as expected. (That's a long story for another time.) And yet God's hand and timing were perfect in it all.

Ringing true to the message of this book, there have been many insecurities to get past, many times of prayer and seeking truth in the Word, and fortunately for me, many people willing to invest and support and cheer on and make this book happen.

For that, many thank-yous are in order.

To James, my steady rock. You always find the best in me and balance me out so well. Through one of the hardest years of your life, you still gave me the space and time to get these words out (while also excelling at everything you're working on). I love you and I'm proud of you.

To my kids, who validate me most as a writer by the way you grab your own notebooks and pencils so you can write books too, just like Mom. You make my heart full. I treasure the moments we celebrated this book together, with delight and dancing, and I'll always celebrate all three of you the same way.

To my family, for being excited with me, especially my mom and dad, who believed in me first. To Jamie, for your impact that lives on through the people you loved.

To Keely, who does all the things: holds my hand through the process, advocates for me, and helps to bring the best words out of me by asking questions and digging deeper. Thanks for taking a chance on me based on one single tweet. I couldn't have asked for a better representative and friend in the publishing world.

To the David C Cook and Esther Press community: Susan, for your faithful vision to empower and equip women in their relationships with God and for being willing to go out on a limb with ordinary people like me. Stephanie, for getting the ball rolling and helping me stay organized. Michael, for your generous feedback, which made me feel like this book just might be worth reading. Judy, for making this book readable and accurate with your keen eye, thoroughness, organization, and kind words. To the design team, the video team, the audio team, everyone I was able to interact with and those who make it happen behind the scenes—thank you.

To such an incredible network of friends who are basically family. Thanks for being patient with me while I dove into writing this and for supporting me even in the days when I didn't know where my writing was going. Elizabeth, thank you for your friendship through this process, for being willing to let me glean from your experience. Desiree, Judith, Briana, Maral, Nicole, Cheryl, Cat, Gaby, Kim, Lauren, Mikaela, and Lindsey (and so many more)—thanks to all of you for keeping me sane.

To the talented women who have gone alongside me in our creative journeys—through writer communities, coaching sessions, internships, and social media—you inspire me, challenge me to think differently, pray with me, and lend me courage. Every interaction, big or small, has left its mark on me.

To the women who have gone before me, sharing faithful messages and examples, knowingly or unknowingly leaving behind lessons and legacies, who taught and affirmed and inspired and challenged me. I'm grateful for you. You're the proof behind the message of this book.

And to every reader, whether you have been with me since my early days of blogging or you just finished this book and it hit home—I've been praying for years for this message to make it to you. Thank you for taking the time to read it.

Notes

Introduction: Know Your Enemy

1. Victoria A. Goodyear and Kathleen M. Armour, eds., *Young People, Social Media and Health* (London: Taylor and Francis, 2019), 48.

2. Goodyear and Armour, *Young People, Social Media and Health*. Specific content was sourced from these pages: low self-worth and self-esteem, 48; depression, 47, 74; eating disorders, 105; unhealthy physical activity, 34; body image issues, 40; see also Andreana Nop, "Young People, Social Media, and Impacts on Well-Being," Clark University (Worcester, MA: School of Professional Studies, 2020), https://commons.clarku.edu/cgi/viewcontent.cgi?article=1046&context=sps_masters_papers; Samantha Ford, "Social Media and Its Implications on Mental Health" (Sacred Heart University, 2021), https://digitalcommons.sacredheart.edu/cgi/viewcontent.cgi?article=1759&context=acadfest.

3. Thomas Curran and Andrew P. Hill, "How Perfectionism Became a Hidden Epidemic among Young People," January 3, 2018, The

Conversation, https://theconversation.com/how-perfectionism-became
-a-hidden-epidemic-among-young-people-89405.

4. Curran and Hill, "How Perfectionism Became a Hidden Epidemic."

5. Prem S. Fry and Dominique L. Debats, "Perfectionism and the Five-Factor Personality Traits as Predictors of Mortality in Older Adults," *Journal of Health Psychology* 14, no. 4 (April 21, 2009), 513–24, https://journals.sagepub.com/doi/10.1177/1359105309103571; see also Sidney J. Blatt, "The Destructiveness of Perfectionism: Implications for the Treatment of Depression," *American Psychologist* 50, no. 12 (1995): 1003–20, https://psycnet.apa.org/doiLanding?doi=10.1037%2F0003-066X.50.12.1003; Gordon L. Flett et al., "Perfectionism, Life Events, and Depressive Symptoms: A Test of a Diathesis-Stress Model," *Current Psychology* 14 (June 1995), 112–37, https://link.springer.com/article/10.1007/BF02686885; Nicholas W. Affrunti and Janet Woodruff-Borden, "Perfectionism in Pediatric Anxiety and Depressive Disorders," *Clinical Child and Family Psychology Review* (January 31, 2014), 299–317, https://link.springer.com/article/10.1007/s10567-014-0164-4; Sarah J. Egan, Tracey D. Wade, and Roz Shafran, "Perfectionism as a Transdiagnostic Process: A Clinical Review," *Clinical Psychology Review* 31, no. 2 (March 2011): 203–12, https://pubmed.ncbi.nlm.nih.gov/20488598.

6. Michelle Chen, "The Issue with Millennials Isn't Narcissism but Our Depressing Culture of Mass Consumption," January 20, 2018, Think, NBC, www.nbcnews.com/think/opinion/issue-millennials-isn-t-narcissism-our-depressing-culture-mass-consumption-ncna839331.

7. Chen, "The Issue with Millennials."

8. Jamie Ballard, "Millennials Are the Loneliest Generation," July 30, 2019, YouGov America, https://today.yougov.com/topics/society/articles-reports /2019/07/30/loneliness-friendship-new-friends-poll-survey.

9. Lydia Denworth, "The Loneliness of the 'Social Distancer' Triggers Brain Cravings Akin to Hunger," *Scientific American*, April 2, 2020, www. scientificamerican.com/article/the-loneliness-of-the-social-distancer -triggers-brain-cravings-akin-to-hunger.

10. Natalie Franke, *Built to Belong: Discovering the Power of Community over Competition* (New York: Worthy Books, 2021), 20.

11. Leon Festinger, "A Theory of Social Comparison Processes," *Human Relations* 7, no. 2 (May 1, 1954): 117–40, www2.psych.ubc.ca/~schaller /528Readings/Festinger1954.pdf; see also Alicia Nortje, "Social Comparison Theory & 12 Real-Life Examples," PositivePsychology.com, April 29, 2020, https://positivepsychology.com/social-comparison.

12. "4089. pikros," *Strong's Concordance*, Bible Hub, accessed March 22, 2023, https://biblehub.com/greek/4089.htm; "2205. zelos," *Strong's Concordance*, Bible Hub, accessed March 22, 2023, https://biblehub.com/greek/2205.htm.

13. "2052. eritheia," *Strong's Concordance*, Bible Hub, accessed March 22, 2023, https://biblehub.com/greek/2052.htm.

14. Luciano Gasser et al., "Emotionally Supportive Classroom Interactions and Students' Perceptions of Their Teachers as Caring and Just," *Learning and Instruction* 54 (April 2018): 82–92; see also Luciano Gasser et al., "Competitive

Classroom Norms and Exclusion of Children with Academic and Behavior Difficulties," *Journal of Applied Developmental Psychology* 49 (March–April 2017): 1–11, sciencedirect.com.

Chapter 1: The Woman Who Doesn't Include You

1. Ming Zhang, Yuqi Zhang, and Yazhuo Kong, "Interaction between Social Pain and Physical Pain," Sage Journals 5, no. 4, May 18, 2020, https://journals .sagepub.com/doi/full/10.26599/BSA.2019.9050023.

2. Melinda French Gates, *The Moment of Lift: How Empowering Women Changes the World* (New York: Flatiron, 2019), 52.

3. Dane Ortlund, *Gentle and Lowly: The Heart of Christ for Sinners and Sufferers* (Wheaton, IL: Crossway, 2020), 179.

Chapter 2: The Woman Who Has What You Want

1. Joshua Brown and Joel Wong, "How Gratitude Changes You and Your Brain," *Greater Good Magazine*, June 6, 2017, https://greatergood.berkeley.edu/article /item/how_gratitude_changes_you_and_your_brain.

2. Ann Voskamp, *One Thousand Gifts: A Dare to Live Fully Right Where You Are* (Grand Rapids, MI: Zondervan, 2010), 45.

Chapter 3: The Woman Who Disagrees with You

1. "1515. eiréné," *Strong's Concordance*, Bible Hub, accessed March 22, 2023, https://biblehub.com/greek/1515.htm.

2. Perry B. Yoder, *Shalom: The Bible's Word for Salvation, Justice, and Peace* (Eugene, OR: Wipf and Stock, 2017), 21–22.

3. Yoder, *Shalom*, 21.

4. Yoder, *Shalom*, 20–21.

5. Yoder, *Shalom*, 21.

6. Osheta Moore, *Shalom Sistas: Living Wholeheartedly in a Brokenhearted World* (Harrisonburg, VA: Herald Press, 2017), 31.

7. Yoder, *Shalom*, 5.

8. Ian Leslie, "A Good Scrap," Aeon, July 12, 2021, https://aeon.co/essays /why-disagreement-is-vital-to-advancing-human-understanding.

Chapter 4: The Woman Whose Suffering Scares You

1. The following resource was helpful for research on Naomi: Phyllis Trible, "Naomi: Bible," Jewish Women's Archive, accessed March 8, 2023, https://jwa.org/encyclopedia/article/naomi-bible.

2. *Sympathy, empathy,* and *compassion* are defined with help from Sara Schairer, "What's the Difference between Empathy, Sympathy, and Compassion?," November 23, 2019, Chopra, https://chopra.com/articles/whats-the-difference -between-empathy-sympathy-and-compassion.

3. Clara Strauss et al., "What Is Compassion and How Can We Measure It? A Review of Definitions and Measures," *Clinical Psychology Review* 47 (July 2016): 15–27, https://psycnet.apa.org/record/2016-33471-003.

4. See, for example, 1 Kings 3:26 NASB.

5. *Strong's Expanded Exhaustive Concordance of the Bible* (Nashville, TN: Thomas Nelson, 2009), s.v. "compassionate"; see also: "Compassion," Bible Project, accessed March 8, 2023, https://bibleproject.com/explore/video/character-of-god-compassion.

6. Sarah E. Fisher, "Rechem/Beten: WOMB-Creation Compassion," Hebrew Word Lessons, November 26, 2017, https://hebrewwordlessons.com/2017/11/26/womb-creation-compassion.

7. "4697. splagchnizomai," *Englishman's Concordance*, Bible Hub, accessed March 22, 2023, https://biblehub.com/greek/4697.htm.

8. *Merriam-Webster Dictionary*, s.v. "indignant," accessed March 22, 2023, www.merriam-webster.com/dictionary/indignant.

9. Fred Rogers, *The World according to Mister Rogers: Important Things to Remember* (New York: Hachette, 2019), 50.

10. See the Grief Recovery Institute, www.griefrecoverymethod.com/our-programs/1-on-1-support.

Chapter 5: The Woman Who Doesn't Believe

1. "Jireh," on Elevation Worship and Maverick City Music, *Old Church Basement*, Elevation Worship, 2021.

2. Priscilla Shirer, *Fervent: A Woman's Battle Plan to Serious, Specific, and Strategic Prayer* (Nashville, TN: B&H, 2015), 268.

3. See "Jesus and the Outcast Woman at the Well," *The Chosen*, season 1, episode 8, aired November 26, 2019, created and directed by Dallas Jenkins, www.youtube.com/watch?v=ordhsDeAt60.

Chapter 6: The Woman Who Has It All Together

1. Natalia Taylor, "I FAKED a vacation at IKEA," YouTube, February 10, 2020, www.youtube.com/watch?v=sz42PrqWq-g.

2. Ben Rector, "The Internet Isn't Real Life," YouTube, December 14, 2021, www.youtube.com/watch?v=mX8o47qRO20&t=14s.

3. Emily McNamara, "Simon," The Bump, accessed March 22, 2023, www.thebump.com/b/simon-baby-name.

4. "Strong's G4613–Simōn," *Thayer's Greek Lexicon*, Bible Hub, accessed March 22, 2023, www.blueletterbible.org/lexicon/g4613/kjv/tr/0-1.

Chapter 7: The Woman Who Has Guardrails Up

1. Ann Voskamp, "Shame Dies When Stories Are Told in Safe Places," Facebook, March 6, 2017, www.facebook.com/AnnVoskamp/photos /maybe-on-the-days-we-want-out-of-our-lives-it-isnt-so-much-that-we-want -to-die-f/1497686953576807/?paipv=0&eav=AfbOeEQFYCaTARsq3Cbw 4I2UoOWQeeKZM0D9_jqbjYaiVY80FDHbzri5GGq9eljPQW0&_rdr. (Emphasis mine.)

2. *Oxford English Dictionary*, s.v. "encouragement," accessed March 21, 2023.

Chapter 8: The Woman Who Is Too Much

1. Nedra Glover Tawwab, *Set Boundaries, Find Peace: A Guide to Reclaiming Yourself* (New York: TarcherPerigree, 2021), xviii.

2. Tawwab, *Set Boundaries, Find Peace*, xviii.

3. Amanda Anderson, "People Pleasing and Boundaries with Amanda Anderson," interview by Jenn Schultz, December 8, 2021, on *Called Into Being,* podcast, 43:44, https://open.spotify.com/episode/0vHqxGyonFD1Jcf0k6sIka ?si=9fdf0e3984154f05.

4. "922. baros," *Thayer's Greek Lexicon*, Bible Hub, accessed March 22, 2023, https://biblehub.com/greek/922.htm.

5. Scot Chadwick, "Contradictions: Bearing Burdens and Loads," Answers in Genesis, September 21, 2015, https://answersingenesis.org/contradictions -in-the-bible/bearing-burdens-and-loads.

6. "5413. phortion," HELPS Word-Studies, Bible Hub, https://biblehub.com/greek/5413.htm; see also Chadwick, "Contradictions," https://answersingenesis.org/contradictions-in-the-bible/bearing-burdens-and-loads.

7. Chadwick, "Contradictions," https://answersingenesis.org/contradictions-in-the-bible/bearing-burdens-and-loads.

Chapter 9: The Woman in the Mirror

1. *Hugo*, directed by Martin Scorsese (Hollywood: Paramount Pictures, 2011).

Conclusion: Embrace the Ongoing Process

1. Amy Poehler, *Yes Please* (New York: Dey Street Books, 2014), 74.

About the Author

Jenn Schultz is a wife, mom, blogger, and podcaster who loves sharing her messy faith story. Growing up in a Christian family and church community, she came to know God. But somewhere along the way she fell for the lie that she was only as loved and accepted as how good she was, and usually found herself falling short. Through a years-long journey of confronting that lie and others with Scripture, she came to the conviction that God frees us to live loved and wholeheartedly through him, right where we are.

She writes on this topic on her blog, *What You Make It*, which has become a solid resource for connection, community, and biblical truths for pursuing a "life to the full," right where God has us. Jenn has grown the community on social media, particularly Instagram, and has also written for *Truly* magazine, *Her View From Home,* and *Today's Parents*; and she has spoken on podcasts and for women's groups. In November 2021, she launched *Called Into Being*, a podcast on stepping confidently into God's purpose for your life and getting rid of the things that get in the way.

estherpress

Our journey invites us deeper into God's Word, where wisdom
waits to renew our minds and where the Holy Spirit meets us in
discernment that empowers bold action for such a time as this.

*If we have the courage to say yes to our calling and
no to everything else, will the world be ready?*

JOIN US IN COURAGEOUS LIVING

Your Esther Press purchase helps to equip, encourage,
and disciple women around the globe with practical assistance
and spiritual mentoring to help them become strong leaders
and faithful followers of Jesus.

An imprint of

transforming lives together